Walter Scott

The Poetical Works

Walter Scott

The Poetical Works

ISBN/EAN: 9783741141683

Manufactured in Europe, USA, Canada, Australia, Japa

Cover: Foto ©Thomas Meinert / pixelio.de

Manufactured and distributed by brebook publishing software
(www.brebook.com)

Walter Scott

The Poetical Works

THE POETICAL WORKS

OF

SIR WALTER SCOTT, BART.

VOL. III.

BORDER MINSTRELSY—III.

EDINBURGH:
ADAM AND CHARLES BLACK.
1861.

MINSTRELSY OF THE SCOTTISH BORDER.

Part II.—Romantic Ballads.

	PAGE
The Douglas Tragedy	8
Young Benjie	10
Lady Anne	18
Lord William	23
The Broomfield Hill	28
Proud Lady Margaret	32
The original ballad of the Broom of the Cowdenknows	37
Lord Randal	43
Sir Hugh Le Blond	51
Græme and Bewick	66
The Duel of Wharton and Stuart. Part First	77
——— Part Second	91
The Lament of the Border Widow	94
Fair Helen of Kirconnell. Part First	98
——— Part Second	103
Hughie the Græme	107
Johnie of Breadislee	114

CONTENTS.

	PAGE
Katharine Janfarie	122
The Laird o' Logie	128
A Lyke-Wake Dirge	135
The Dowie Dens of Yarrow	143
The Gay Goss-Hawk	151
Brown Adam	159
Jollon Grame	162
Willie's Ladye	168
Clerk Saunders	175
Earl Richard	184
The Dæmon Lover	194
The Lass of Lochroyan	199
Rose the Red and White Lilly	208
Fause Foodrage	220
Kempion	230
Lord Thomas and Fair Annie	249
The Wife of Usher's Well	258
Cospatrick	263
Prince Robert	269
King Henrie	274
Annan Water	282
The Cruel Sister	287
The Queen's Marie	294
The Bonny Hynd	307
O gin my Love were yon Red Rose	313
O tell me how to woo thee	315
The Souters of Selkirk	317
The Flowers of the Forest. Part First	338
——————— Part Second	336
The Laird of Muirhead	341
Ode on Visiting Flodden	343

MINSTRELSY

OF THE

SCOTTISH BORDER:

CONSISTING OF

HISTORICAL AND ROMANTIC BALLADS,

COLLECTED

IN THE SOUTHERN COUNTIES OF SCOTLAND; WITH A FEW
OF MODERN DATE, FOUNDED UPON
LOCAL TRADITION.

> The songs, to savage virtue dear,
> That won of yore the public ear,
> Ere polity, sedate and sage,
> Had quench'd the fires of feudal rage.
> 					WARTON.

THE DOUGLAS TRAGEDY.

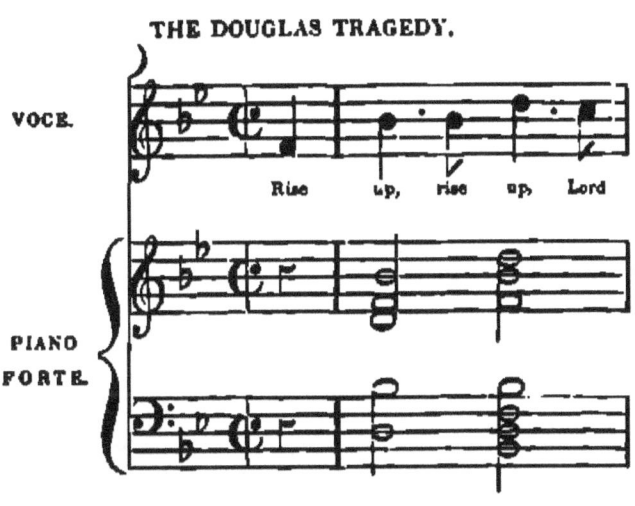

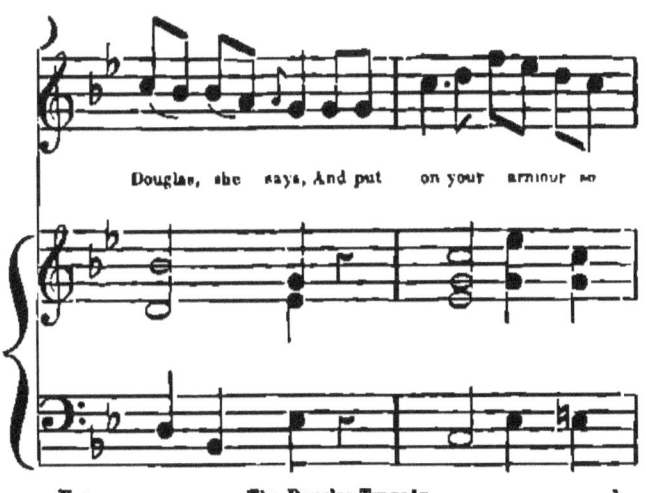

THE DOUGLAS TRAGEDY, CONTINUED.

bright, Let it ne--ver be said that a daughter of thine Was married to a Lord under

THE DOUGLAS TRAGEDY, CONTINUED.

THE DOUGLAS TRAGEDY.

The ballad of *The Douglas Tragedy* is one of the few, to which popular tradition has ascribed complete locality.

The farm of Blackhouse, in Selkirkshire, is said to have been the scene of this melancholy event. There are the remains of a very ancient tower, adjacent to the farmhouse, in a wild and solitary glen, upon a torrent, named Douglas burn, which joins the Yarrow, after passing a craggy rock, called the Douglas craig. This wild scene, now a part of the Traquair estate, formed one of the most ancient possessions of the renowned family of Douglas; for Sir John Douglas, eldest son of William, the first Lord Douglas, is said to have sat, as baronial lord of Douglas burn, during his father's lifetime, in a parliament of Malcolm Canmore, held at Forfar.—GODSCROFT, vol. i. p. 20.

The tower appears to have been square, with a circular turret at one angle, for carrying up the staircase, and for flanking the entrance. It is said to have derived its name of Blackhouse from the complexion of the Lords of Douglas, whose swarthy hue was a family attribute. But, when the high mountains, by which it is enclosed, were covered with heather, which was the case till of late years, Blackhouse must also have merited its appellation from the appearance of the scenery.

From this ancient tower, Lady Margaret is said to have been carried by her lover. Seven large stones, erected upon the neighbouring heights of Blackhouse, are shown, as marking the spot where the seven brethren were slain; and the Douglas burn is averred to have been the stream, at which the lovers stopped to drink: so minute is tradition in ascertaining the scene of a tragical tale, which, considering the rude state of former times, had probably foundation in some real event.

Many copies of this ballad are current among the vulgar, but chiefly in a state of great corruption; especially such as have been committed to the press in the shape of penny pamphlets. One of these is now before me, which, among many others, has the ridiculous error of " *blue gilded* horn," for " *bugelet* horn." The copy, principally used in this edition of the ballad, was supplied by Mr Sharpe.[1] The three last verses are given from the printed copy, and from tradition. The hackneyed verse, of the rose and the brier springing from the grave of the lovers, is common to most tragic ballads; but it is introduced into this with singular propriety, as the chapel of St Mary, whose

[1] [Charles Kirkpatrick Sharpe, Esq.]

vestiges may be still traced upon the lake to which it
has given name, is said to have been the burial-place
of Lord William and Fair Margaret. The wrath of
the Black Douglas, which vented itself upon the brier,
far surpasses the usual stanza:—

> " At length came the clerk of the parish,
>   As you the truth shall hear,
> And by mischance he cut them down,
>   Or else they had still been there."[1]

[1] [At the time when Sir Walter Scott was collecting the materials for this work, the farm of Blackhouse was tenanted by the father of his attached friend, and in latter days factor, (or land-steward,) Mr William Laidlaw. James Hogg was shepherd on the same farm, and in the course of one of his exploring rides up the glen of Yarrow, Sir Walter made acquaintance with young Laidlaw and the "Mountain Bard," who both thenceforth laboured with congenial zeal in behalf of his undertaking. —Ed.]

THE DOUGLAS TRAGEDY.

"Rise up, rise up, now, Lord Douglas," she says,
  "And put on your armour so bright;
Let it never be said that a daughter of thine
  Was married to a lord under night.

"Rise up, rise up, my seven bold sons,
  And put on your armour so bright,
And take better care of your youngest sister,
  For your eldest's awa' the last night."—

He's mounted her on a milk-white steed,
  And himself on a dapple grey,
With a bugelet horn hung down by his side,
  And lightly they rode away.

Lord William lookit o'er his left shoulder,
  To see what he could see,
And there he spy'd her seven brethren bold,
  Come riding o'er the lee.

"Light down, light down, Lady Marg'ret," he said,
  "And hold my steed in your hand,

Until that against your seven brethren bold,
   And your father, I make a stand."—

She held his steed in her milk-white hand,
   And never shed one tear,
Until that she saw her seven brethren fa',
   And her father hard fighting, who loved her so dear.

" O hold your hand, Lord William!" she said,
   " For your strokes they are wondrous sair;
True lovers I can get many a ane,
   But a father I can never get mair."—

O, she's ta'en out her handkerchief,
   It was o' the holland sae fine,
And aye she dighted[1] her father's bloody wounds,
   That were redder than the wine.

" O chuse, O chuse, Lady Marg'ret," he said,
   " O whether will ye gang or bide?"—
" I'll gang, I'll gang, Lord William," she said,
   " For you have left me no other guide."—

He's lifted her on a milk-white steed,
   And himself on a dapple grey,
With a bugelet horn hung down by his side,
   And slowly they baith rade away.

[1] *Dighted*—Wiped.

O they rade on, and on they rade,
   And a' by the light of the moon,
Until they came to yon wan water,
   And there they lighted down.

They lighted down to tak a drink
   Of the spring that ran sae clear;
And down the stream ran his gude heart's blood,
   And sair she 'gan to fear.

" Hold up, hold up, Lord William," she says,
   " For I fear that you are slain!"—
" 'Tis naething but the shadow of my scarlet cloak,
   That shines in the water sae plain."—

O they rade on, and on they rade,
   And a' by the light of the moon,
Until they cam to his mother's ha' door,
   And there they lighted down.

" Get up, get up, lady mother," he says,
   " Get up, and let me in!—
Get up, get up, lady mother," he says,
   " For this night my fair lady I've win.

" O mak my bed, lady mother," he says,
   " O mak it braid and deep!
And lay Lady Marg'ret close at my back,
   And the sounder I will sleep."—

Lord William was dead lang ere midnight,
    Lady Marg'ret lang ere day—
And all true lovers that go thegither,
    May they have mair luck than they!

Lord William was buried in St Marie's kirk,
    Lady Marg'ret in Marie's quire;
Out o' the lady's grave grew a bonny red rose,
    And out o' the knight's a brier.

And they twa met, and they twa plat,
    And fain they wad be near;
And a' the warld might ken right weel,
    They were twa lovers dear.

But bye and rade the Black Douglas,
    And wow but he was rough!
For he pull'd up the bonny brier,
    And flang'd in St Marie's Loch.[1]

[1] [Mr Motherwell gives in his "Minstrelsy," 1827, a copy of this ballad as usually recited in the *West* of Scotland; but the variations it supplies are trivial, and all for the worse.—ED.]

YOUNG BENJIE.

NEVER BEFORE PUBLISHED.

In this ballad the reader will find traces of a singular superstition, not yet altogether discredited in the wilder parts of Scotland. The lykewake, or watching a dead body, in itself a melancholy office, is rendered, in the idea of the assistants, more dismally awful, by the mysterious horrors of superstition. In the interval betwixt death and interment, the disembodied spirit is supposed to hover around its mortal habitation, and, if invoked by certain rites, retains the power of communicating, through its organs, the cause of its dissolution. Such enquiries, however, are always dangerous, and never to be resorted to, unless the deceased is suspected to have suffered *foul play*, as it is called. It is the more unsafe to tamper with this charm in an unauthorized manner, because the inhabitants of the infernal regions are, at such periods, peculiarly active. One of the most potent ceremonies in the charm, for causing the dead body to speak, is, setting the door ajar, or half open. On this account, the peasants of Scotland sedulously avoid leaving the door ajar, while a corpse lies in the house. The door must either be left wide open, or quite shut; but the first is always preferred, on account of the exercise of hospitality usual on such occasions. The attendants must be likewise careful never to leave the corpse for a moment alone, or, if it is left alone, to avoid, with a degree of superstitious horror, the first sight of it.

The following story, which is frequently related by the peasants of Scotland, will illustrate the imaginary danger of leaving the door ajar. In former times, a man and his wife lived in a solitary cottage, on one of the extensive Border fells. One day the husband died suddenly; and his wife, who was equally afraid of staying alone by the corpse, or leaving the dead body by itself, repeatedly went to the door, and looked anxiously over the lonely moor for the sight of some person approaching. In her confusion and alarm she accidentally left the door ajar, when the corpse suddenly started up, and sat in the bed, frowning and grinning at her frightfully. She sat alone, crying bitterly, unable to avoid the fascination of the dead man's eye, and too much terrified to break the sullen silence, till a Catholic priest, passing over the wild, entered the cottage. He first set the door quite open, then put his little finger in his mouth, and said the paternoster backwards; when the horrid look of the corpse relaxed, it fell back on the bed, and behaved itself as a dead man ought to do.

The ballad is given from tradition. I have been informed by a lady,[1] of the highest literary eminence, that she has heard a ballad on the same subject, in which the scene was laid upon the banks of the Clyde. The chorus was,

"O Bothwell banks bloom bonny,"

and the watching of the dead corpse was said to have taken place in Bothwell church.

[1] [Miss Joanna Baillie—who was born at Long-Calderwood near Bothwell.—ED.]

YOUNG BENJIE.

Of a' the maids o' fair Scotland,
 The fairest was Marjorie;
And young Benjie was her ae true love,
 And a dear true love was he.

And wow but they were lovers dear,
 And loved fu' constantlie;
But aye the mair when they fell out,
 The sairer was their plea.[1]

And they hae quarrell'd on a day,
 Till Marjorie's heart grew wae;
And she said she'd chuse another luve,
 And let young Benjie gae.

And he was stout,[2] and proud-hearted,
 And thought o't bitterlie;
And he's gane by the wan moonlight,
 To meet his Marjorie.

[1] *Plea*—Used obliquely for *dispute*.
[2] *Stout*, through this whole ballad, except in one instance, (stanza 10,) signifies *haughty*.

"O open, open, my true love,
    O open, and let me in!"—
"I darena open, young Benjie,
    My three brothers are within."—

"Ye lied, ye lied, ye bonny burd,
    Sae loud's I hear ye lie;
As I came by the Lowden banks,
    They bade gude e'en to me.

"But fare ye weel, my ae fause love,
    That I have loved sae lang!
It sets ye¹ chuse another love,
    And let young Benjie gang."—

Then Marjorie turn'd her round about,
    The tear blinding her ee,—
"I darena, darena let thee in,
    But I'll come down to thee."—

Then saft she smiled, and said to him,
    "O what ill hae I done?"—
He took her in his armis twa,
    And threw her o'er the linn.

The stream was strang, the maid was stout,
    And laith laith to be dang,²

¹ *Sets ye*—Becomes you—ironical.—² *Dang*—Defeated.

But, ere she wan the Lowden banks,
　Her fair colour was wan.

Then up bespak her eldest brother,
　"O see na ye what I see?"—
And out then spak her second brother,
　"It's our sister Marjorie!"—

Out then spak her eldest brother,
　"O how shall we her ken?"—
And out then spak her youngest brother,
　"There's a honey mark on her chin."—

Then they've ta'en up the comely corpse,
　And laid it on the ground—
"O wha has killed our ae sister,
　And how can he be found?

"The night it is her low lykewake,
　The morn her burial day,
And we maun watch at mirk midnight,
　And hear what she will say."—

Wi' doors ajar, and candle light,
　And torches burning clear,
The streikit corpse, till still midnight,
　They waked, but naething hear.

About the middle o' the night,
　　The cocks began to craw;
And at the dead hour o' the night,
　　The corpse began to thraw.

"O whae has done the wrang, sister,
　　Or dared the deadly sin?
Whae was sae stout, and fear'd nae dout,
　　As thraw ye o'er the linn?"—

"Young Benjie was the first ae man
　　I laid my love upon;
He was sae stout, and proud-hearted,
　　He threw me o'er the linn."—

"Sall we young Benjie head, sister,
　　Sall we young Benjie hang,
Or sall we pike out his twa gray een,
　　And punish him ere he gang?"—

"Ye maunna Benjie head, brothers,
　　Ye maunna Benjie hang,
But ye maun pike out his twa gray een,
　　And punish him ere he gang.

"Tie a green gravat round his neck,
　　And lead him out and in,
And the best ae servant about your house
　　To wait young Benjie on.

THE SCOTTISH BORDER.

" And aye, at every seven years' end,
 Ye'll tak him to the linn;
For that's the penance he maun dree,
 To scug[1] his deadly sin."—

[1] *Scug*—Shelter, or expiate.

LADY ANNE.

This ballad was communicated to me by Mr Kirkpatrick Sharpe of Hoddom, who mentions having copied it from an old magazine. Although it has probably received some modern corrections, the general turn seems to be ancient, and corresponds with that of a fragment, containing the following verses, which I have often heard sung in my childhood:—

> "She set her back against a thorn,
> And there she has her young son born;
> 'O smile nae sae, my bonny babe!
> An ye smile sae sweet, ye'll smile me dead.'—
> * * * * *
> An' when that lady went to the church,
> She spied a naked boy in the porch.
>
> "'O bonny boy, an ye were mine,
> I'd clead ye in the silks sae fine.'—
> 'O mother dear, when I was thine,
> To me ye were na half sae kind.'"[1]

Stories of this nature are very common in the annals of popular superstition. It is, for example, currently

[1] [Mr Motherwell has received, from recitation in the west of Scotland, a fuller, and less poetical, copy of this piece—

believed in Ettrick Forest, that a libertine, who had destroyed fifty-six inhabited houses, in order to throw the possessions of the cottagers into his estate, and who added, to this injury, that of seducing their daughters, was wont to commit to a carrier in the neighbourhood the care of his illegitimate children, shortly after they were born. His emissary regularly carried them away, but they were never again heard of. The unjust and cruel gains of the profligate laird were dissipated by his extravagance, and the ruins of his house seem to bear witness to the truth of the rhythmical prophecies denounced against it, and still current among the peasantry. He himself died an untimely death; but the agent of his amours and crimes survived to extreme old age. When on his death-bed, he seemed much oppressed in mind, and sent for a clergyman to speak

> " She leaned her back unto a thorn,
> And there she has her two babes born.
> She took frae 'bout her ribbon belt,
> And there she bound them hand and foot.
> She has ta'en out her wee penknife,
> And there she ended baith their life," &c.
> *Minstrelsy*, 1827, p. 161.

But Mr Buchan produces what he considers as a perfect edition. See his second volume, p. 222, " The Cruel Mother." One verse will show how the burden is introduced:—

> " She's howkit a hole anent the meen, Edinbro', Edinbro',
> She's howkit a hole anent the meen, Stirling for aye;
> She's howkit a hole anent the meen,
> There laid her sweet baby in;
> So proper Saint Johnstown stands fair upon Tay."—Ed.]

peace to his departing spirit: but, before the messenger returned, the man was in his last agony; and the terrified assistants had fled from his cottage, unanimously averring, that the wailing of murdered infants had ascended from behind his couch, and mingled with the groans of the departing sinner.

LADY ANNE.

Fair Lady Anne sate in her bower,
  Down by the greenwood side,
And the flowers did spring, and the birds did sing,
  'Twas the pleasant May-day tide.

But fair Lady Anne on Sir William call'd,
  With the tear grit in her ee,
" O though thou be fause, may Heaven thee guard,
  In the wars ayont the sea!"—

Out of the wood came three bonnie boys,
  Upon the simmer's morn,
And they did sing and play at the ba',
  As naked as they were born.

" O seven lang years wad I sit here,
  Amang the frost and snaw,
A' to hae but ane o' these bonnie boys,
  A playing at the ba'."—

Then up and spake the eldest boy,
  " Now listen, thou fair ladie,

And ponder well the rede that I tell,
　Then make ye a choice of the three.

" 'Tis I am Peter, and this is Paul,
　And that ane, sae fair to see,
But a twelve-month sinsyne to paradise came,
　To join with our companie."—

" O I will hae the snaw-white boy,
　The bonniest of the three."—
" And if I were thine, and in thy propine,[1]
　O what wad ye do to me?"—

" 'Tis I wad clead thee in silk and gowd,
　And nourice thee on my knee."—
" O mither! mither! when I was thine,
　Sic kindness I couldna see.

" Beneath the turf, where now I stand,
　The fause nurse buried me;
The cruel penknife sticks still in my heart,
　And I come not back to thee."—

* 　* 　* 　* 　* 　* 　*

[1] *Propine*—Usually gift, but here the power of giving or bestowing.

LORD WILLIAM.

This ballad was communicated to me by Mr James Hogg; and, although it bears a strong resemblance to that of *Earl Richard*,[1] so strong, indeed, as to warrant a supposition that the one has been derived from the other, yet its intrinsic merit seems to warrant its insertion. Mr Hogg has added the following note, which, in the course of my enquiries, I have found amply corroborated:—

"I am fully convinced of the antiquity of this song; for, although much of the language seems somewhat modernized, this must be attributed to its currency, being much liked, and very much sung in this neighbourhood. I can trace it back several generations, but cannot hear of its ever having been in print. I have never heard it with any considerable variation, save that one reciter called the dwelling of the feigned sweetheart, *Castleswa*."

[1] [See this ballad, *post*.]

LORD WILLIAM.

Lord William was the bravest knight
   That dwalt in fair Scotland,
And though renown'd in France and Spain,
   Fell by a ladie's hand.

As she was walking maid alone,
   Down by yon shady wood,
She heard a smit[1] o' bridle reins,
   She wish'd might be for good.

" Come to my arms, my dear Willie,
   You're welcome hame to me ;
To best o' cheer and charcoal red,[2]
   And candle burning free."—

---

[1] *Smit*—Clashing noise, from smite—hence also (*perhaps*) Smith and Smithy.

[2] *Charcoal red*—This circumstance marks the antiquity of the poem. While wood was plenty in Scotland, charcoal was the usual fuel in the chambers of the wealthy.

" I winna light, I darena light,
　　Nor come to your arms at a';
A fairer maid than ten o' you
　　I'll meet at Castle-law."—

" A fairer maid than me, Willie!
　　A fairer maid than me!
A fairer maid than ten o' me
　　Your eyes did never see."—

He louted[1] ower his saddle lap,
　　To kiss her ere they part,
And wi' a little keen bodkin,
　　She pierced him to the heart.

" Ride on, ride on, Lord William now,
　　As fast as ye can dree!
Your bonny lass at Castle-law
　　Will weary you to see."—

Out up then spake a bonny bird,
　　Sat high upon a tree,—
" How could you kill that noble lord?
　　He came to marry thee."—

" Come down, come down, my bonny bird,
　　And eat bread aff my hand!

[1] *Louted*—Stooped.

Your cage shall be of wiry goud,
    Whar now it's but the wand."—

" Keep ye your cage o' goud, lady,
    And I will keep my tree;
As ye hae done to Lord William,
    Sae wad ye do to me."—

She set her foot on her door step,
    A bonny marble stane;
And carried him to her chamber,
    O'er him to make her mane.

And she has kept that good lord's corpse
    Three quarters of a year,
Until that word began to spread,
    Then she began to fear.

Then she cried on her waiting maid,
    Aye ready at her ca';
" There is a knight into my bower,
    'Tis time he were awa."—

The ane has ta'en him by the head,
    The ither by the feet,
And thrown him in the wan water,
    That ran baith wide and deep.

"Look back, look back, now, lady fair,
 On him that lo'ed ye weel!
A better man than that blue corpse
 N'er drew a sword of steel."—

THE BROOMFIELD HILL.

The concluding verses of this ballad were inserted in the copy of *Tamlane*, given to the public in the first edition of this work. They are now restored to their proper place. Considering how very apt the most accurate reciters are to patch up one ballad with verses from another, the utmost caution cannot always avoid such errors.

A more sanguine antiquary than the Editor might perhaps endeavour to identify this poem, which is of undoubted antiquity, with the "*Broom Broom on Hill,*" mentioned by Lane, in his *Progress of Queen Elizabeth into Warwickshire*, as forming part of Captain Cox's collection, so much envied by the black-letter antiquaries of the present day.—Dugdale's *Warwickshire*, p. 166. The same ballad is quoted by one of the personages, in a "very merry and pythic comedie," called, "*The longer thou livest, the more Fool thou art.*" See Ritson's Dissertation prefixed to *Ancient Songs*, p. lx. "Brume brume on hill" is also mentioned in the *Complaynt of Scotland*. See Leyden's edition, p. 100.

THE BROOMFIELD HILL.

There was a knight and a lady bright
   Had a true tryst[1] at the broom;
The ane ga'ed early in the morning,
   The other in the afternoon.

And aye she sat in her mother's bower door,
   And aye she made her mane,
" O whether should I gang to the Broomfield hill,
   Or should I stay at hame?

" For if I gang to the Broomfield hill,
   My maidenhead is gone;
And if I chance to stay at hame,
   My love will ca' me mansworn."—

Up then spake a witch woman,
   Aye from the room aboon;
" O, ye may gang to Broomfield hill,
   And yet come maiden hame.

---

[1] *Tryst*—Assignation.

" For when ye come to the Broomfield hill,
  Ye'll find your love asleep,
With a silver belt about his head,
  And a broom-cow[1] at his feet.

" Take ye the blossom of the broom;
  The blossom it smells sweet,
And strew it at your true love's head,
  And likewise at his feet.

" Take ye the rings off your fingers,
  Put them on his right hand,
To let him know, when he doth awake,
  His love was at his command."—

She pu'd the broom flower on Hive-hill,
  And strew'd on's white hals bane,[2]
And that was to be wittering true,
  That maiden she had gane.

" O where were ye, my milk-white steed,
  That I hae coft[3] sae dear,
That wadna watch and waken me,
  When there was maiden here?"—

---

[1] *A broom-cow*—A bush of broom.
[2] *Hals*—Neck. (German.)
[3] *Coft*—Bought. From the same root, are the old English *cheap*, i. e. market; German, *Kauffman*, i. e. merchant; *Kopenhagen*, the merchant's haven, &c. &c.

" I stamped wi' my foot, master,
 And gar'd my bridle ring;
But nae kin' thing wald waken ye,
 Till she was past and gane."—

" And woe betide ye, my gay goss hawk,
 That I did love sae dear,
That wadna watch and waken me,
 When there was maiden here."—

" I clapped wi' my wings, master,
 And aye my bells I rang,
And aye cry'd, Waken, waken, master,
 Before the ladye gang."—

" But haste and haste, my gude white steed,
 To come the maiden till,
Or a' the birds of gude green wood
 Of your flesh shall have their fill."—

" Ye needna burst your gude white steed,
 Wi' racing o'er the howm;[1]
Nae bird flies faster through the wood,
 Than she fled through the broom."

[1] *Howm*, or *holm*—a flat ground by a river.

PROUD LADY MARGARET.

This ballad was communicated to the Editor by Mr Hamilton, *Music-seller, Edinburgh, with whose mother it had been a favourite. Two verses and one line were wanting, which are here supplied from a different Ballad, having a plot somewhat similar. These verses are the 6th and 9th.*

'Twas on a night, an evening bright,
   When the dew began to fa',
Lady Margaret was walking up and down,
   Looking o'er her castle wa'.

She looked east, and she looked west,
   To see what she could spy,
When a gallant knight came in her sight,
   And to the gate drew nigh.

" You seem to be no gentleman,
   You wear your boots so wide;
But you seem to be some cunning hunter,
   You wear the horn so syde."—[1]

[1] *Syde*—Long or low.

" I am no cunning hunter," he said,
    " Nor ne'er intend to be ;
But I am come to this castle
    To seek the love of thee ;
And if you do not grant me love,
    This night for thee I'll die."—

" If you should die for me, sir knight,
    There's few for you will mane,
For mony a better has died for me,
    Whose graves are growing green.

" But ye maun read my riddle," she said,
    " And answer me questions three ;
And but ye read them right," she said,
    " Gae stretch ye out and die.—

" Now what is the flower, the ae first flower,
    Springs either on moor or dale ;
And what is the bird, the bonnie bonnie bird,
    Sings on the evening gale ? "—

" The primrose is the ae first flower
    Springs either on moor or dale ;
And the thristlecock is the bonniest bird
    Sings on the evening gale."—

" But what's the little coin," she said,
    " Wald buy my castle bound ?

And what's the little boat," she said,
"Can sail the world all round?"—

" O hey, how mony small pennies
Make thrice three thousand pound?
Or hey, how many small fishes
Swim n' the salt sea round?"—

" I think ye maun be my match," she said,
"My match and something mair,
You are the first e'er got the grant
Of love frae my father's heir.

" My father was lord of nine castles,
My mother lady of three;
My father was lord of nine castles,
And there's nane to heir but me.

" And round about a' thae castles,
You may baith plow and saw,
And on the fifteenth day of May
The meadows they will maw."—

" O hald your tongue, Lady Margaret," he said,
" For loud I hear you lie!
Your father was lord of nine castles,
Your mother was lady of three;
Your father was lord of nine castles,
But ye fa' heir to but three.

" And round about a' thae castles,
  You may baith plow and saw,
But on the fifteenth day of May
  The meadows will not maw.

" I am your brother Willie," he said,
  " I trow ye ken na me ;
I came to humble your haughty heart,
  Has gar'd sae mony die."—

" If ye be my brother Willie," she said,
  " As I trow weel ye be,
This night I'll neither eat nor drink,
  But gae along wi' thee."—

" O hald your tongue, Lady Margaret," he said,
  " Again I hear you lie ;
For ye've unwashen hands, and ye've unwashen feet,[1]
  To gae to clay wi' me.

" For the wee worms are my bedfellows,
  And cauld clay is my sheets ;
And when the stormy winds do blow,
  My body lies and sleeps."[2]

---

[1] *Unwashen hands and unwashen feet*—Alluding to the custom of washing and dressing dead bodies.

[2] [In Mr Buchan's Collection, vol. i. p. 31, there is a north-country edition of this ballad, under the title of " The Courteous Knight." His is, as usual, a coarse and vulgar version ; but it con-

tains many more stanzas than that in the text; and the knight's farewell speech runs into an edifying lecture on his sister's vanity of dress: *e. g.*

> " My body's buried in Dumfermline,
>   And far beyont the sea,
> But day nor night nae rest could get
>   All for the pride o' thee:
>
> " When ye are in the gude kirk set,
>   The gowd pins in your hair,
> Ye tak mair delight in your feckless dress
>   Than ye do in the morning prayer," &c.—ED.]

THE

ORIGINAL BALLAD

OF

THE BROOM OF COWDENKNOWS.

The beautiful air of Cowdenknows is well known and popular. In Ettrick Forest the following words are uniformly adapted to the tune, and seem to be the original ballad. An edition of this pastoral tale, differing considerably from the present copy, was published by Mr HERD, *in* 1772. *Cowdenknows is situated upon the Leader, about four miles from Melrose, and is now the property of* Dr HOME.

O THE broom, and the bonny bonny broom,
    And the broom of the Cowdenknows!
And aye sae sweet as the lassie sang,
    I' the bought, milking the ewes.

The hills were high on ilka side,
    An' the bought i' the lirk[1] o' the hill,
And aye, as she sang, her voice it rang,
    Out o'er the head o' yon hill.

[1] *Lirk*—Hollow.

There was a troop o' gentlemen
    Came riding merrilie by,
And one of them has rode out o' the way,
    To the bought to the bonny may.

" Weel may ye save an' see, bonny lass,
    An' weel may ye save an' see."—
" An' sae wi' you, ye weel-bred knight,
    And what's your will wi' me?"—

" The night is misty and mirk, fair may,
    And I have ridden astray,
And will you be so kind, fair may,
    As come out and point my way?"—

" Ride out, ride out, ye ramp rider!
    Your steed's baith stout and strang;
For out of the bought I dare na come,
    For fear 'at ye do me wrang."—

" O winna ye pity me, bonny lass,
    O winna ye pity me?
An' winna ye pity my poor steed,
    Stands trembling at yon tree?"—

" I wadna pity your poor steed,
    Though it were tied to a thorn;
For if ye wad gain my love the night,
    Ye wad slight me ere the morn.

" For I ken you by your weel-busket hat,
   And your merrie twinkling ee,
That ye're the Laird o' the Oakland hills,
   An' ye may weel seem for to be."—

" But I am not the Laird o' the Oakland hills,
   Ye're far mista'en o' me;
But I'm ane o' the men about his house,
   An' right aft in his companie."—

He's ta'en her by the middle jimp,
   And by the grass-green sleeve;
He's lifted her over the fauld-dyke,
   And speer'd at her sma' leave.

O he's ta'en out a purse o' gowd,
   And streek'd her yellow hair,
" Now, take ye that, my bonny may,
   Of me till you hear mair."—

O he's leapt on his berry-brown steed,
   An' soon he's o'erta'en his men;
And ane and a' cried out to him,
   " O master, ye've tarry'd lang!"—

" O I hae been east, and I hae been west,
   An' I hae been far o'er the knowes,
But the bonniest lass that ever I saw
   Is i' the bought, milking the ewes."—

She set the cog¹ upon her head,
    An' she's gane singing hame—
"O where hae ye been, my ae daughter?
    Ye hae na been your lane."—

"O naebody was wi' me, father,
    O naebody has been wi' me;
The night is misty and mirk, father,
    Yee may gang to the door and see.

"But wae be to your ewe-herd, father,
    And an ill deed may he die;
He bug² the bought at the back o' the knowe,
    And a tod³ has frighted me.

"There came a tod to the bought door,
    The like I never saw;
And ere he had ta'en the lamb he did,
    I had lourd⁴ he had ta'en them a'."— .

O whan fifteen weeks was come and gane,
    Fifteen weeks and three,
That lassie began to look thin and pale,
    An' to long for his merry-twinkling ee.

It fell on a day, on a het simmer day,
    She was ca'ing out her father's kye,

¹ *Cog*—Milking-pail.—² *Bug*—Built.—³ *Tod*—Fox.
⁴ *Lourd*—Liefer.

Bye came a troop o' gentlemen,
  A' merrilie riding bye.

" Weel may ye save an' see, bonny may,
  Weel may ye save and see!
Weel I wat, ye be a very bonny may,
  But whae's aught that babe ye are wi' ?"—

Never a word could that lassie say,
  For never a ane could she blame,
An' never a word could the lassie say,
  But " I have a gudeman at hame."—

" Ye lied, ye lied, my very bonny may,
  Sae loud as I hear you lie;
For dinna ye mind that misty night
  I was i' the bought wi' thee?

" I ken you by your middle sae jimp,
  An' your merry-twinkling ee,
That ye're the bonny lass i' the Cowdenknow,
  An' ye may weel seem for to be."—

Then he's leapt off his berry-brown steed,
  An' he's set that fair may on—
" Ca' out your kye, gude father, yoursell,
  For she's never ca' them out again.

"I am the Laird of the Oakland hills,
  I hae thirty plows and three;
An' I hae gotten the bonniest lass
  That's in a' the south countrie."

LORD RANDAL.

THERE is a beautiful air to this old ballad. The hero is more generally termed *Lord Ronald;* but I willingly follow the authority of an Ettrick Forest copy for calling him *Randal;* because, though the circumstances are so very different, I think it not impossible, that the ballad may have originally regarded the death of Thomas Randolph, or Randal, Earl of Murray, nephew to Robert Bruce, and governor of Scotland. This great warrior died at Musselburgh, 1332, at the moment when his services were most necessary to his country, already threatened by an English army. For this sole reason, perhaps, our historians obstinately impute his death to poison. See *The Bruce,* Book xx. Fordun repeats, and Boece echoes, this story, both of whom charge the murder on Edward III. But it is combated successfully by Lord Hailes, in his *Remarks on the History of Scotland.*

The substitution of some venomous reptile for food, or putting it into liquor, was anciently supposed to be a common mode of administering poison; as appears from the following curious account of the death of

King John, extracted from a MS. Chronicle of England, *penes* John Clerk, Esq. advocate.[1] " And, in the same tyme, the pope sente into Englond a legate, that men cald Swals, and he was prest cardinal of Rome, for to mayntene King Johnes cause agens the barons of Englond; but the barons had so much pte [*poustie*, i. e. power] through Lewys, the kinges sone of Fraunce, that Kinge Johne wist not wher for to wend ne gone: and so hitt fell, that he wold have gone to Suchold, and as he went thedurward, he come by the abbey of Swinshed, and ther he abode 11 dayes. And, as he sato at meat, he askyd a monke of the house, how moche a lofe was worth, that was before hym sete at the table? and the monke sayd that loffe was worthe bot ane half-penny. 'O!' quod the Kyng, 'this is a grette cheppe of brede; now,' said the king, 'and yff I may, such a loffe shall be worth xxd. or half a yer be gone:' and when he said the word, muche he thought, and ofte tymes sighed, and nome and ete of the bred, and said, 'By Gode, the word that I have spokyn shall be sothe.' The monke, that stode before the kyng, was ful sory in his hert; and thought rather he wold himself suffer peteous deth; and thought yff he myght ordeyn therfore sum remedy. And anon the monke went unto his abbott, and was schryvyd of him, and told the abbott all that the kyng said, and prayed his abbott to assoyl him, for he wold gyffe the kyng such a wassayle, that

[1] [Mr Clerk became a judge of the Court of Session by the title of Lord Eldin, and died in 1831.—ED.]

all England shuld be glad and joyful therof. Tho went the monke into a gardene, and fonde a tode therin; and toke her upp, and put hyr in a cuppe, and filled it with good ale, and pryked hyr in every place, in the cuppe, till the venome come out in every place; an brought hitt befor the kyng, and knelyd, and said, 'Sir, wassayle; for never in your lyfe drancke ye of such a cuppe.'—'Begyne, monke,' quod the king; and the monke dranke a gret draute, and toke the kyng the cuppe, and the kyng also drank a grett draute, and set downe the cuppe.—The monke anon went to the Farmarye, and ther dyed anone, on whose soule God have mercy, Amen. And v monkes syng for his soule especially, and shall while the abbey stondith. The kyng was anon ful evil at ese, and comaunded to remove the table, and askyd aftur the monke; and men told him that he was ded, for his wombe was broke in sondur. When the king herd this tidyng, he comaundyd for to trusse; but all hit was for nought, for his bely began to swelle for the drink that he dranke, that he dyed within 11 days, the moro aftur Seynt Luke's day."

A different account of the poisoning of King John is given in a MS. Chronicle of England, written in the minority of Edward III., and contained in the Auchinleck MS. of Edinburgh. Though not exactly to our present purpose, the passage is curious, and I shall quote it without apology. The author has mentioned the interdict laid on John's kingdom by the Pope, and continues thus:—

" He was ful wroth and grim,
For no prest wald sing for him.
He made tho his parlement,
And swore his *croy de verament*,
That he shuld make such assaut,
To fede all Inglonde with a spand,
And eke with a white lof,
Therefore I hope[1] he was God-loth.
A monk it herd of Swines heued,
And of his wordes he was adred,
He went hym to his fere,
And seyd to hem in this maner:
'The King has made a sori oth,
That he schal with a white lof
Fede al Inglonde, and with a spand,
Y wis it were a sori saut
And better is that we die to,
Than al Inglond be so wo.
Ye schul for me belles ring,
And after wordes rede and sing;
So helpe you God, heven King,
Granteth me alle now min asking,
And Ichim wil with puseoun slo,
Ne shall he never Inglond do wo.'

" His brethren him graunt alle his bone,
He let him shrive swithe sone,
To make his soule fair and clene,
To for our leued i heven queen,
That schs schuld for him be,
To for her son in trinité.

" Dansimond sede and gadred frut,
For sothe were plommes white,
The steles[2] he puld out evirichon,
Puisoun he dede therin anon,

[1] *Hope*, for *think*.— [2] *Steles*—Stalks.

And sett the steles al ogyn,
That the gile schuld nought be sen.
He dede hem in a coupe of gold,
And went to the kinges bord ;
On knee he him sett,
The king full fair he grett ;
' Sir,' he said, ' by Seynt Austin,
This is frout of our garden,
And gif that your wil be,
Assayet herof after me.'
Dansimond ete frut, on and on,
And al tho other ete King Jon ;
The monk aros, and went his way,
God gif his soule wel gode day ;
He gaf King Jon ther his puisoun,
Himself had that ilk doun,
He dede, it is nouther for mirthe ne ond,
Bot for to save al Inglond.

"The King Jon sats at mete,
His wombe to wex grete ;
He swore his oath, *per la croyde*,
His wombe wald brest a thre ;
He wald have risen fram the bord
Ac he ne spake never more word :
Thus ended his time,
Y wis he had an evel fine."

Shakspeare, from such old Chronicles, has drawn his authority for the last fine scene in *King John*. But he probably had it from Caxton, who uses nearly the words of the prose chronicle. Hemingford tells the same tale with the metrical historian. It is certain, that John increased the flux, of which he died, by the intemperate use of peaches and of ale, which may have given rise to the story of the poison.—See MATTHEW PARIS.

To return to the ballad; there is a very similar song, in which, apparently to excite greater interest in the nursery, the handsome young hunter is exchanged for a little child, poisoned by a false step-mother.[1]

[1] [This nursery song is probably that inserted in Buchan's Collection, 1828, vol. ii. p. 179—" *Willie Doo*," i.e. *dove :*

"Where hae ye been a' day,
Willie Doo, Willie Doo?
Whare hae ye been a' day,
Willie, my doo?

"I've been to see my stepmother,
Mak my bed, lay me down;
Mak my bed, lay me down,
Die shall I now," &c.—ED.]

LORD RANDAL.

"O where hae ye been, Lord Randal, my son?
O where hae ye been, my handsome young man?"—
"I hae been to the wild wood; mother, make my bed
  soon,
For I'm weary wi' hunting, and fain wald lie down."—

"Where gat ye your dinner, Lord Randal, my son?
Where gat ye your dinner, my handsome young man?"—
"I dined wi' my true-love; mother, make my bed soon,
For I'm weary wi' hunting, and fain wald lie down."—

"What gat ye to your dinner, Lord Randal, my son?
What gat ye to your dinner, my handsome young
  man?"—
"I gat eels boil'd in broo; mother, make my bed soon,
For I'm weary wi' hunting, and fain wald lie down."—

"What became of your bloodhounds, Lord Randal, my
  son?
What became of your bloodhounds, my handsome young
  man?"—

"O they swell'd and they died; mother, make my bed
  soon,
For I'm weary wi' hunting, and fain wald lie down."—

"O I fear ye are poison'd, Lord Randal, my son!
O I fear ye are poisoned, my handsome young man!"—
"O yes! I am poison'd; mother, make my bed soon,
For I'm sick at the heart, and I fain wad lie down."[1]

---

[1] [In the edition of this ballad published by Mr Kinloch in 1827, the name of the hero is *Lord Donald*—very natural in a north country version. The youth is poisoned by a dish of *toads*, served up as fish, to which the Editor thinks we owe the Scotch phrase, of "getting frogs for fish "—*i.e.* foul play—introduced in the subsequent ballad of *Katharine Janfarie*. The last verse is—

"What will ye leave to your true love, Lord Donald, my son
What will ye leave to your true love, my jollie young man?"—
"The tow and the halter for to hang on yon tree,
And let her hang there for the poysoning o' me."—P. 113—ED.]

SIR HUGH LE BLOND.

This ballad is a northern composition, and seems to have been the original of the legend called *Sir Aldingar*, which is printed in the *Reliques of Ancient Poetry*. The incidents are nearly the same in both ballads, excepting that, in *Aldingar*, an angel combats for the queen, instead of a mortal champion. The names of *Aldingar* and *Rodingham* approach near to each other in sound, though not in orthography, and the one might, by reciters, be easily substituted for the other. I think I have seen both the name and the story in an ancient prose chronicle, but am unable to make any reference in support of my belief.

The tradition, upon which the ballad is founded, is universally current in the Mearns; and the Editor is informed, that, till very lately, the sword, with which Sir Hugh le Blond was believed to have defended the life and honour of the Queen, was carefully preserved by his descendants, the Viscounts of Arbuthnot. That Sir Hugh of Arbuthnot lived in the thirteenth century, is proved by his having, 1282, bestowed the patronage of the church of Garvoch upon the Monks of Aberbrothwick, for the safety of his soul.—*Register of Aberbrothwick, quoted by Crawford in Peerage.* But I find no instance in history, in which the honour of a Queen of Scotland was committed to the chance of a duel. It is true, that Mary, wife of Alexander II., was, about 1242, somewhat implicated in a dark story, concerning the murder of Patrick, Earl of Athole, burned in his lodging at Haddington, where he had gone to attend a great tournament. The relations of the deceased baron accused of the murder Sir William Bisat, a powerful nobleman, who appears to have been in such high favour with the young Queen, that she offered her oath, as a compurgator, to prove his innocence. Bisat himself stood upon his defence, and proffered the combat to his accusers; but he was obliged to give way to the tide, and was banished from Scotland. This affair interested all the northern barons; and it is not impossible, that some share, taken in it by this Sir Hugh de Arbuthnot, may have given a slight foundation for the tradition of the country.— WINTOUN, book vii. ch. 9. Or, if we suppose Sir Hugh le Blond to be a predecessor of the Sir Hugh who flourished in the thirteenth century, he may have been the victor in a duel, shortly noticed as having occurred in 1154, when one Arthur, accused of treason, was unsuccessful in his appeal to the judgment of God. *Arthurus regem Malcolm proditurus duello periit.* Chron. Sanctæ Crucis, ap. Anglia Sacra, vol. i. p. 161.

But, true or false, the incident narrated in the ballad, is in the genuine style of chivalry. Romances abound with similar instances, nor are they wanting in real history. The most solemn part of a knight's oath was to defend "all widows, orphelines, and maidens of gude fame."[1]—LINDSAY's *Heraldry, MS.* The love of arms was a real passion of itself, which blazed yet more fiercely when united with the enthusiastic admiration of the fair sex. The Knight of Chaucer exclaims, with chivalrous energy,

> "To fight for a lady! a benedicite!
> It were a lusty sight for to see."

It was an argument, seriously urged by Sir John of Heinault, for making war upon Edward II. in behalf of his banished wife, Isabella, that knights were bound to aid, to their uttermost power, all distressed damsels, living without counsel or comfort.

An apt illustration of the ballad would have been the combat undertaken by three Spanish champions against three Moors of Grenada, in defence of the honour of the Queen of Grenada, wife to Mohommed Chiquito, the last

---

[1] Such an oath is still taken by the Knights of the Bath; but, I believe, few of that honourable brotherhood will now consider it quite so obligatory as the conscientious Lord Herbert of Cherbury, who gravely alleges it as a sufficient reason for having challenged divers cavaliers, that they had either snatched from a lady her bouquet, or ribbon, or by some discourtesy of similar importance, placed her, as his lordship conceived, in the predicament of a distressed damozell.

monarch of that kingdom. But I have not at hand *Las Guerras Civiles de Granada*, in which that achievement is recorded. Raymond Berenger, Count of Barcelona, is also said to have defended, in single combat, the life and honour of the Empress Matilda, wife of the Emperor Henry V., and mother to Henry II. of England.—See ANTONIO ULLOA, *del vero Honore Militare*, Venice, 1569.

A less apocryphal example is the duel, fought in 1387, betwixt Jaques le Grys and John de Carogne, before the King of France. These warriors were retainers of the Earl of Alençon, and originally sworn brothers. John de Carogne went over the sea, for the advancement of his fame, leaving in his castle a beautiful wife, where she lived soberly and sagely. But the devil entered into the heart of Jaques le Grys, and he rode, one morning, from the Earl's house to the castle of his friend, where he was hospitably received by the unsuspicious lady. He requested her to show him the donjon, or keep of the castle, and in that remote and inaccessible tower forcibly violated her chastity. He then mounted his horse, and returned to the Earl of Alençon within so short a space, that his absence had not been perceived. The lady abode within the donjon, weeping bitterly, and exclaiming, " Ah, Jaques! it was not well done thus to shame me! but on you shall the shame rest, if God send my husband safe home!" The lady kept secret this sorrowful deed until her husband's return from his voyage. The day passed, and night came, and the knight went to bed; but the lady would not; for ever she blessed herself, and walked up and down the chamber, studying and musing, until her attendants had retired; and then, throwing herself on her knees before the knight, she showed him all the adventure. Hardly would Carogne believe the treachery of his companion: but, when convinced, he replied, " Since it is so, lady, I pardon you; but the knight shall die for this villanous deed." Accordingly, Jacques le Grys was accused of the crime in the court of the Earl of Alençon. But, as he was greatly loved of his lord, and as the evidence was very slender, the Earl gave judgment against the accusers. Hereupon John Curogne appealed to the Parliament of Paris; which court, after full consideration, appointed the case to be tried by mortal combat betwixt the parties, John Carogne appearing as the champion of his lady. If he failed in his combat, then was he to be hanged, and his lady burnt, as false and unjust calumniators. This combat, under circumstances so very peculiar, attracted universal attention; in so much, that the King of France and his peers, who were then in Flanders collecting troops for an invasion of England, returned to Paris, that so notable a duel might be fought in the royal presence.

" Thus," says Froissart, " the Kynge, and his uncles, and the constable, came to Parys. Then the lystes were made in a place called Saynt Katheryne, behinde the Temple. There was so moche people, that it was merrayle to beholde; and on the one side of the lystes there was made gret scaffoldes, that the lordes might the better se the batayle of the ii champions; and so they bothe came to the felde, armed at all peaces, and there eche of them was set in theyr chayre; the Erle of Saynt Poule gouverned John Carongne, and Erle of Alanson's company with Jacques le Grys; and when the knyght entred in to the felde, he came to his wyfe, who was there syttynge in a chayre, covered in blacke, and he sayd to her thus:—' Dame, by your informacyon, and in your quarrell, I do put my lyfe in adventure, as to fyght with Jacques le Grys; ye knowe, if the cause be just and true.'—' Syr,' said the lady, ' it is as I have sayd; wherefore ye maye fight surely; the cause is good and true.' With those wordes, the knyghte kissed the lady, and toke her by the hande, and then blessed hym, and soo entred into the felde. The lady sate styll in the blacke chayre, in her prayers to God, and to the Vyrgyne Mary, humbly prayenge them, by theyr specyall grace, to send her husband the victory, accordynge to the ryght. She was in gret hevynes, for she was not sure of her lyfe; for, if her husbande sholde have ben discomfyted, she was judged, without remedy to be brente, and her husbande hanged. I cannot say whether she repented her or not, as the matter was so forwarde, that both she and her husbande were in grete peryll: howbeit, fynally, she must as then abyde the adventure. Then these two champyons were set one against another, and so mount-

ed on theyr horses, and behauved them nobly; for they
knewe what perteyned to deedes of armes. There were
many lordes and knyghtes of Fraunce, that were come
thyder to se that batayle. The two champyons justed
at theyr fyrst metyng, but none of them did hurte
other; and after the justes, they lyghted on foote to
perfourme theyr batayle, and soo fought valyauntly.—
And fyrst, John of Carongne was hurt in the thyghe,
whereby all his frendes were in grete fere; but, after
that, he fought so valyauntly, that he betto down his
adversary to the erthe, and threst his swerd in his body,
and soo slew hym in the felde; and then demanded, if
he had done his devoyre or not? and they answered,
that he had valyauntly atchieved his batayle. Then
Jacques le Grys was delyuered to the hangman of Parys,
and he drewe hym to the gybbet of Mountfawcon, and
there hanged him up. Then John of Carongne came
before the kynge, and kneled downe, and the kynge
made him to stand up before hym; and, the same daye,
the kynge caused to be delyvered to hym a thousande
franks, and reteyned him to be of his chambre, with a
pencyon of ii hundred pounde by yere, durynge the
term of his lyfe. Then he thanked the kynge and the
lordes, and went to his wyfe, and kissed her; and then
they wente togyder to the chyrche of Our Ladye, in
Parys, and made theyr offerynge, and then retourned
to theyr lodgynges. Then this Sir John of Carongne
taryed not longe in Fraunce, but went, with Syr John
Boucequant, Syr John of Bordes, and Syr Loys Grat.

All these went to se Lamorabaquyn,[1] of whome, in those dayes, there was moche spekynge."

Such was the readiness, with which, in those times, heroes put their lives in jeopardy, for honour and lady's sake. But I doubt whether the fair dames of the present day will think, that the risk of being burnt, upon every suspicion of frailty, would be altogether compensated by the probability, that a husband of good faith, like John de Carogne, or a disinterested champion, like Hugh le Blond, would take up the gauntlet in their behalf. I fear they will rather accord to the sentiment of the hero of an old romance, who expostulates thus with a certain duke:—

> "Certes, Sir Duke, thou doest unright,
> To make a roast of your daughter bright,
> I wot you ben unkind."
> *Amis and Amelion.*

I was favoured with the following copy of *Sir Hugh le Blond*, by K. Williamson Burnet, Esq. of Monboddo, who wrote it down from the recitation of an old woman, long in the service of the Arbuthnot family. Of course, the diction is very much humbled, and it has, in all probability, undergone many corruptions; but its antiquity is indubitable, and the story, though indifferently told, is in itself interesting. It is believed, that there have been many more verses.

[1] This name Froissart gives to the famous Mahomet, Emperor of Turkey, called the Great. It is a corruption of his Persian title, Ameer Uddeen Kawn.

SIR HUGH LE BLOND.

The birds sang sweet as ony bell,
  The world had not their make,[1]
The Queen she's gone to her chamber,
  With Rodingham to talk.

" I love you well, my Queen, my dame,
  'Bove land and rents so clear,
And for the love of you, my Queen,
  Would thole pain most severe."—

" If well you love me, Rodingham,
  I'm sure so do I thee:
I love you well as any man,
  Save the King's fair bodye."—

" I love you well, my Queen, my dame;
  'Tis truth that I do tell:
And for to lye a night with you,
  The salt seas I would sail."—

[1] *Make*—Equal.

" Away, away, O Rodingham!
    You are both stark and stoor;
Would you defile the King's own bed,
    And make his Queen a whore?

" To-morrow you'd be taken sure,
    And like a traitor slain;
And I'd be burned at a stake,
    Although I be the Queen."—

He then stepp'd out at her room door,
    All in an angry mood:
Until he met a leper-man,[1]
    Just by the hard way-side.

He intoxicate the leper-man,
    With liquors very sweet:
And gave him more and more to drink,
    Until he fell asleep.

He took him in his armis twa,
    And carried him along,
Till he came to the Queen's own bed,
    And there he laid him down.

---

[1] Filth, poorness of living, and the want of linen, made this horrible disease formerly very common in Scotland. Robert Bruce died of the leprosy; and, through all Scotland, there were hospitals erected for the reception of lepers, to prevent their mingling with the rest of the community.

He then stepp'd out of the Queen's bower,
    As swift as any roe,
'Till he came to the very place
    Where the King himself did go.

The King said unto Rodingham,
    " What news have you to me ?"—
He said, " Your Queen's a false woman,
    As I did plainly see."—

He hasten'd to the Queen's chamber,
    So costly and so fine,
Until he came to the Queen's own bed,
    Where the leper-man was lain.

He looked on the leper-man,
    Who lay on his Queen's bed;
He lifted up the snow-white sheets,
    And thus he to him said :—

" Plooky, plooky,[1] are your cheeks,
    And plooky is your chin,
And plooky are your armis twa,
    My bonny Queen's layne in.

" Since she has lain into your arms,
    She shall not lye in mine;

---

[1] *Plooky*—pimpled.

Since she has kiss'd your ugsome mouth,
    She never shall kiss mine."—

In anger he went to the Queen,
    Who fell upon her knee;
He said, " You false, unchaste woman,
    What's this you've done to me?"—

The Queen then turn'd herself about,
    The tear blinded her ee—
" There's not a knight in a' your court
    Dare give that name to me."—

He said, " 'Tis true that I do say;
    For I a proof did make:
You shall be taken from my bower,
    And burned at a stake.

" Perhaps I'll take my word again,
    And may repent the same,
If that you'll get a Christian man
    To fight that Rodingham."—

" Alas! alas!" then cried our Queen,
    " Alas, and woe to me!
There's not a man in all Scotland
    Will fight with him for me."—

She breathed unto her messengers,
    Sent them south, east, and west;

They could find none to fight with him,
    Nor enter the contest.

She breathed on her messengers,
    She sent them to the north;
And there they found Sir Hugh le Blond,
    To fight him he came forth.

When unto him they did unfold
    The circumstance all right,
He bade them go and tell the Queen,
    That for her he would fight.

The day came on that was to do
    That dreadful tragedy:
Sir Hugh le Blond was not come up
    To fight for our ladye.

" Put on the fire," the monster said:
    " It is twelve on the bell."—[1]

---

[1] In the romance of Doolin, called '*La Fleurs des Battailles*, a false accuser discovers a similar impatience to hurry over the execution, before the arrival of the lady's champion:—" *Ainsi comme Herchambaut vouloit jetter la dame dedans le feu, Sanxes de Clervaut va a lui, et lui dict : ' Sire Herchambaut, vous estes trop à blasmer ; car vous ne devez mener ceste chose que par droit ainsi qu'il est ordonné ; je veux accorder que ceste dame ait un vassal qui la diffendra contre vous et Drouart, car elle n'a point de coulpe en ce que l'accusex ; si la devez retarder jusque a midy, pour scavoir si un bon chevalier l'a viendra secourir contre vous et Drouart.'* "—Cap. 22.

"'Tis scarcely ten, now," said the King;
"I heard the clock mysell."—

Before the hour the Queen is brought,
   The burning to proceed;
In a black velvet chair she's set,
   A token for the dead.

She saw the flames ascending high,
   The tears blinded her ee:
"Where is the worthy knight," she said,
"Who is to fight for me?"—

Then up and spak the King himsell,
   "My dearest, have no doubt,
For yonder comes the man himsell,
   As bold as e'er set out."—

They then advanced to fight the duel
   With swords of temper'd steel,
Till down the blood of Rodingham
   Came running to his heel.

Sir Hugh took out a lusty sword,
   'Twas of the metal clear,
And he has pierced Rodingham
   Till's heart-blood did appear.

"Confess your treachery, now," he said,
"This day before you die!"—

"I do confess my treachery,
  I shall no longer lye:

"I like to wicked Haman am,
  This day I shall be slain."—
The Queen was brought to her chamber,
  A good woman again.

The Queen then said unto the King,
  "Arbattle's near the sea;
Give it unto the northern knight,
  That this day fought for me."—

Then said the King, "Come here, Sir Knight,
  And drink a glass of wine;
And, if Arbattle's not enough,
  To it we'll Fordoun join."[1]

[1] Arbattle is the ancient name of the barony of Arbuthnot—Fordun has long been the patrimony of the same family.

GRÆME AND BEWICK.

The date of this ballad, and its subject, are uncertain. From internal evidence, I am inclined to place it late in the sixteenth century. Of the Græmes enough is elsewhere said. It is not impossible, that such a clan, as they are described, may have retained the rude ignorance of ancient Border manners to a later period than their more inland neighbours; and hence the taunt of old Bewick to Græme. Bewick is an ancient name in Cumberland and Northumberland. The ballad itself was given, in the first edition, from the recitation of a gentleman, who professed to have forgotten some verses. These have, in the present edition, been partly restored, from a copy obtained by the recitation of an ostler in Carlisle, which has also furnished some slight alterations.

The ballad is remarkable, as containing, probably, the very latest allusion to the institution of brotherhood in arms, which was held so sacred in the days of chivalry, and whose origin may be traced up to the Scythian ancestors of Odin. Many of the old romances turn entirely upon the sanctity of the engagement, contracted by the *freres d'armes.* In that of *Amis and Amelion,* the hero slays his two infant children, that he may compound a potent salve with their blood, to cure the leprosy of his brother-in-arms. The romance of *Gyron le Courtois* has a similar subject. I think the hero, like Græme in the ballad, kills himself, out of some high point of honour towards his friend.

The quarrel of the two old chieftains, over their wine, is highly in character. Two generations have not elapsed since the custom of drinking deep, and taking deadly revenge for slight offences, produced very tragical events on the Border; to which the custom of going armed to festive meetings contributed not a little. A minstrel, who flourished about 1720, and is often talked of by the old people, happened to be performing before one of these parties, when they betook themselves to their swords. The cautious musician, accustomed to such scenes, dived beneath the table. A moment after, a man's hand, struck off with a back-sword, fell beside him. The minstrel secured it carefully in his pocket, as he would have done any other loose movable; sagely observing, the owner would miss it sorely next morning. I choose rather to give this ludicrous example, than some graver instances of bloodshed at Border orgies. I observe it is said in a MS. account of Tweeddale, in praise of the inhabitants, that, " when they fall in the humour of good fellowship, they use it as a cement and bond of society, and not to foment revenge, quarrels, and murders, which is usual in other counties;" by which we ought, probably, to understand Selkirkshire and Teviotdale.—*Macfarlane's MSS.*

GRÆME AND BEWICK.

Gude Lord Græme is to Carlisle gane;
  Sir Robert Bewick there met he;
And arm in arm to the wine they did go,
  And they drank till they were baith merrie.

Gude Lord Græme has ta'en up the cup,
  " Sir Robert Bewick, and here's to thee!
And here's to our twae sons at hame!
  For they like us best in our ain countrie."—

" O were your son a lad like mine,
  And learn'd some books that he could read,
They might hae been twae brethren bauld,
  And they might hae bragged the Border side.

" But your son's a lad, and he is but bad,
  And billie to my son he canna be;
    *   *   *   *

" Ye sent him to the schools, and he wadna learn;
  Ye bought him books, and he wadna read."—

"But my blessing shall he never earn,
   Till I see how his arm can defend his head."—

Gude Lord Græme has a reckoning call'd,
   A reckoning then called he;
And he paid a crown, and it went roun';
   It was all for the gude wine and free.[1]

And he has to the stable gane,
   Where there stude thirty steeds and three:
He's ta'en his ain horse amang them a',
   And hame he rade sae manfullie.

"Welcome, my auld father!" said Christie Græme,
   "But where sae lang frae hame were ye?"—
"It's I hae been at Carlisle town,
   And a baffled man by thee I be.

"I hae been at Carlisle town,
   Where Sir Robert Bewick he met me;
He says ye're a lad, and ye are but bad,
   And billie to his son ye canna be.

"I sent ye to the schools, and ye wadna learn;
   I bought ye books, and ye wadna read;
Therefore my blessing ye shall never earn,
   Till I see with Bewick thou save thy head."—

[1] The ostler's copy reads very characteristically,
"It was all for good wine and hay."

" Now, God forbid, my auld father,
    That ever sic a thing suld be !
Billie Bewick was my master, and I was his scholar,
    And aye sae weel as he learned me."—

" O hald thy tongue, thou limmer loon,
    And of thy talking let me be !
If thou does na end me this quarrel soon,
    There is my glove, I'll fight wi' thee."—

Then Christie Græme he stooped low
    Unto the ground, you shall understand ;—
" O father, put on your glove again,
    The wind has blown it from your hand ?"—

" What's that thou says, thou limmer loon ?
    How dares thou stand to speak to me ?
If thou do not end this quarrel soon,
    There's my right hand thou shalt fight with me."—

Then Christie Græme's to his chamber gane,
    To consider weel what then should be ;
Whether he should fight with his auld father,
    Or with his billie Bewick, he.

" If I suld kill my billie dear,
    God's blessing I shall never win ;
But if I strike at my auld father,
    I think 'twald be a mortal sin.

"But if I kill my billie dear,
    It is God's will, so let it be;
But I make a vow, ere I gang frae hame,
    That I shall be the next man's die."—

Then he's put on's back a gude auld jack,
    And on his head a cap of steel,
And sword and buckler by his side;
    O gin he did not become them weel!

We'll leave off talking of Christie Græme,
    And talk of him again belive;[1]
And we will talk of bonny Bewick,
    Where he was teaching his scholars five.

When he had taught them well to fence,
    And handle swords without any doubt,
He took his sword under his arm,
    And he walk'd his father's close about.

He look'd atween him and the sun,
    And a' to see what there might be,
Till he spied a man in armour bright,
    Was riding that way most hastilie.

"O wha is yon, that came this way,
    Sae hastilie that hither came?
I think it be my brother dear!
    I think it be young Christie Græme.—

[1] *Belive*—By and by.

" Ye're welcome here, my billie dear,
   And thrice ye're welcome unto me ! "—
" But I'm wae to say, I've seen the day,
   When I am come to fight wi' thee.

" My father's gane to Carlisle town,
   Wi' your father Bewick there met he :
He says I'm a lad, and I am but bad,
   And a baffled man I trow I be.

" He sent me to schools, and I wadna learn ;
   He gae me books, and I wadna read ;
Sae my father's blessing I'll never earn,
   Till he see how my arm can guard my head."—

" O God forbid, my billie dear,
   That ever such a thing suld be!
We'll take three men on either side,
   And see if we can our fathers agree."—

" O hald thy tongue, now, billie Bewick,
   And of thy talking let me be !
But if thou'rt a man, as I'm sure thou art,
   Come o'er the dyke, and fight wi' me."—

" But I hae nae harness, billie, on my back,
   As weel I see there is on thine."—
" But as little harness as is on thy back,
   As little, billie, shall be on mine."—

Then he's thrown aff his coat o' mail
  His cap of steel away flung he;
He stuck his spear into the ground,
  And he tied his horse unto a tree.

Then Bewick has thrown aff his cloak,
  And's psalter-book frae's hand flung he;
He laid his hand upon the dyke,
  And ower he lap most manfullie.

O they hae fought for twae lang hours;
  When twae lang hours were come and gane,
The sweat drapp'd fast frae aff them baith,
  But a drap of blude could not be seen.

Till Græme gae Bewick an ackward[1] stroke,
  Ane ackward stroke strucken sickerlie;
He has hit him under the left breast,
  And dead-wounded to the ground fell he.

"Rise up, rise up, now, billie dear!
  Arise and speak three words to me!—
Whether thou's gotten thy deadly wound,
  Or if God and good leeching may succour thee?"—

"O horse, O horse, now, billie Græme,
  And get thee far from hence with speed;

[1] *Ackward*—Backward.

And get thee out of this country,
    That none may know who has done the deed."—

" O I have slain thee, billie Bewick,
    If this be true thou tellest to me;
But I made a vow, ere I came frae hame,
    That aye the next man I wad be."

He has pitch'd his sword in a moodie-hill,[1]
    And he has leap'd twenty lang feet and three,
And on his ain sword's point he lap,
    And dead upon the ground fell he.

'Twas then came up Sir Robert Bewick,
    And his brave son alive saw he;
" Rise up, rise up, my son," he said,
    " For I think ye hae gotten the victorie."—

" O hald your tongue, my father dear!
    Of your prideful talking let me be!
Ye might hae drunken your wine in peace,
    And let me and my billie be.

" Gae dig a grave, baith wide and deep,
    And a grave to hald baith him and me;
But lay Christie Græme on the sunny side,
    For I'm sure he wan the victorie."—

[1] *Moodie-hill*—Mole-hill.

"Alack! a wae!" auld Bewick cried,
 "Alack! was I not much to blame?
I'm sure I've lost the liveliest lad
 That e'er was born unto my name."—

"Alack! a wae!" quo' gude Lord Græme—
 "I'm sure I hae lost the deeper lack!
I durst hae ridden the Border through,
 Had Christie Græme been at my back.

"Had I been led through Liddesdale,
 And thirty horsemen guarding me,
And Christie Græme been at my back,
 Sae soon as he had set me free!

"I've lost my hopes, I've lost my joy,
 I've lost the key but and the lock;
I durst hae ridden the world round,
 Had Christie Græme been at my back."

THE

DUEL OF WHARTON AND STUART.

IN TWO PARTS.

Duels, as may be seen from the two preceding ballads, are derived from the times of chivalry. They succeeded to the *combat at outrance*, about the end of the sixteenth century; and, though they were no longer countenanced by the laws, nor considered a solemn appeal to the Deity, nor honoured by the presence of applauding monarchs and multitudes, yet they were authorized by the manners of the age, and by the applause of the fair.[1] They long continued, they even yet con-

---

[1] " All things being ready for the ball, and every one being in their place, and I myself being next to the Queen (of France), expecting when the dancers would come in, one knocks at the door somewhat louder than became, as I thought, a very civil person. When he came in, I remember there was a sudden whisper among the ladies, saying, ' C'est Monsieur Balagny,' or, 'Tis Monsieur Balagny ; whereupon, also, I saw the ladies and gentlemen, one after another, invite him to sit near them ; and, which is more, when one lady had his company a while, another would say, ' You have enjoyed him long enough ; I must have him now ;' at which bold civility of theirs, though I were astonished, yet it added unto my

tinue, to be appealed to as the test of truth; since, by the code of honour, every gentleman is still bound to repel a charge of falsehood with the point of his sword, and at the peril of his life.

This peculiarity of manners, which would have surprised an ancient Roman, is obviously deduced from the

> wonder, that his person could not be thought, at most, but ordinary handsome; his hair, which was cut very short, half grey, his doublet but of sackcloth, cut to his shirt, and his breeches only of plain grey cloth. Informing myself of some standers-by who he was, I was told he was one of the gallantest men in the world, as having killed eight or nine men in single fight; and that, for this reason, the ladies made so much of him; it being the manner of all French women to cherish gallant men, as thinking they could not make so much of any one else, with the safety of their honour."—*Life of Lord Herbert of Cherbury*, p. 70. How near the character of the duellist, originally, approached to that of the knight-errant, appears from a transaction which took place at the siege of Juliers, betwixt this Balagny and Lord Herbert. As these two noted duellists stood together in the trenches, the Frenchman addressed Lord Herbert: "*Monsieur, on dit que vous êtes un des plus braves de votre nation, et je suis Balagny; allons voir qui fera le mieux.*" With these words, Balagny jumped over the trench, and Herbert as speedily following, both ran sword in hand towards the defences of the besieged town, which welcomed their approach with a storm of musketry and artillery. Balagny then observed this was hot service, but Herbert swore he would not turn back first; so the Frenchman was finally fain to set him the example of retreat. Notwithstanding the advantage which he had gained over Balagny, in this "jeopardy of war," Lord Herbert seems still to have grudged that gentleman's astonishing reputation; for he endeavoured to pick a quarrel with him, on the romantic score of the worth of their mistresses; and, receiving a ludicrous answer, told him, with disdain, that he spoke more like a *palliard* than a *cavalier*. From such instances, the reader may judge, whether the age of chivalry did not endure somewhat longer than is generally supposed.

Gothic ordeal of trial by combat. Nevertheless, the custom of duelling was considered, at its first introduction, as an innovation upon the law of arms; and a book, in two huge volumes, entitled *Le vrai Theatre d'Honneur et de la Chivalerie*, was written by a French nobleman, to support the venerable institutions of chivalry against this unceremonious mode of combat. He has chosen for his frontispiece two figures; the first represents a conquering knight, trampling his enemy under foot in the lists, crowned by Justice with laurel, and preceded by Fame, sounding his praises. The other figure presents a duellist, in his shirt, as was then the fashion, (see the following ballad,) with his bloody rapier in his hand: the slaughtered combatant is seen in the distance, and the victor is pursued by the Furies. Nevertheless, the wise will make some scruple, whether, if the warriors were to change equipments, they might not also exchange their emblematic attendants.

The modern mode of duel without defensive armour, began about the reign of Henry III. of France, when the gentlemen of that nation, as we learn from Davila, began to lay aside the cumbrous lance and cuirass, even in war. The increase of danger being supposed to contribute to the increase of honour, the national ardour of the French gallants led them early to distinguish themselves by neglect of every thing that could contribute to their personal safety. Hence, duels began to be fought by the combatants in their shirts, and with the rapier only. To this custom contributed also the art of fencing, then cultivated as a new study in Italy and Spain, by which the sword became at once an offensive and defensive weapon. The reader will see the new "science of defence," as it was called, ridiculed by Shakspeare, in *Romeo and Juliet*, and by Quevedo, in some of his novels. But the more ancient customs continued for some time to maintain their ground. The Sieur Colombiere mentions two gentlemen, who fought with equal advantage for a whole day, in all the panoply of chivalry, and, the next day, had recourse to the modern mode of combat. By a still more extraordinary mixture of ancient and modern fashions, two combatants on horseback ran a tilt at each other with lances, without any covering but their shirts.

When armour was laid aside, the consequence was, that the first duels were very sanguinary, terminating frequently in the death of one, and sometimes, as in the ballad, of both persons engaged. Nor was this all: the seconds, who had nothing to do with the quarrel, fought stoutly, *pour se desennuyer*, and often sealed with their blood their friendship for their principals. A desperate combat, fought between Messrs Entraguet and Caylus, is said to have been the first, in which this fashion of promiscuous fight was introduced. It proved fatal to two of Henry the Third's minions, and extracted from that sorrowing monarch an edict against duelling, which was as frequently as fruitlessly renewed by his successors. The use of rapier and poniard together,[1] was another cause of the mortal slaughter in these duels, which were supposed, in the reign of Henry IV., to have cost France at least as many of her nobles as had fallen in the civil wars. With these double weapons, frequent instances occurred, in which a duellist, mortally wounded, threw himself within his antagonist's guard, and plunged his poniard into his heart. Nay, sometimes the sword was altogether abandoned for the more sure and murderous dagger. A quarrel having arisen betwixt the Vicomte d'Allemagne and the Sieur de la Roque, the former, alleging the youth and dexterity of his antagonist, insisted upon fighting the duel in their shirts, and with their poniards only; a desperate mode of conflict, which proved fatal to both. Others refined even upon this horrible struggle, by choosing for the scene a small room, a large hogshead, or, finally, a hole dug in the earth, into which the duellists descended, as into a certain grave. Must I add, that even women caught the frenzy, and that duels were fought, not only by those whose rank and character rendered it little surprising, but by modest and well-born maidens!—*Audiguier Traité de Duel. Theatre D'Honneur*, vol. i.[2]

---

[1] It appears from a line in the black-letter copy of the following ballad, that Wharton and Stuart fought with rapier and dagger:—
"With that stout Wharton was the first
Took *rapier* and *poniard* there that day."
Ancient Songs, 1792, p. 204.

[2] This folly ran to such a pitch, that no one was thought worthy

We learn, from every authority, that duels became nearly as common in England, after the accession of James VI., as they had ever been in France. The point of honour, so fatal to the gallants of the age, was nowhere carried more highly than at the court of the pacific *Solomon* of Britain. Instead of the feudal combats, upon the *Hiegate of Edinburgh*, which had often disturbed his repose at Holyrood, his levees, at Theobald's, were occupied with listening to the detail of more polished, but not less sanguinary, contests. I rather suppose, that James never was himself disposed to pay particular attention to the laws of the *duello;* but they were defined with a quaintness and pedantry, which, bating his dislike to the subject, must have deeply interested him. The point of honour was a science, which a grown gentleman might study under suitable professors, as well as dancing, or any other modish accomplishment. Nay, it would appear, that the ingenuity of the *sword-men* (so these military casuists were termed) might often accommodate a bashful combatant with an honourable excuse for declining the combat:—

to be reckoned a gentleman, who had not tried his valour in at least one duel; of which Lord Herbert gives the following instance: A young gentleman, desiring to marry a niece of Monsieur Disancour, ecuyer to the Duke de Montmorenci, received this answer: " Friend, it is not yet time to marry; if you will be a brave man, you must first kill, in single combat, two or three men; then marry, and get two or three children; otherwise the world will neither have gained nor lost by you."—HERBERT's *Life*, p. 64.

>   —" Understand'st thou well nice points of duel?
>   Art born of gentle blood and pure descent?
>   Were none of all thy lineage hang'd, or cuckold?
>   Bastard or bastinadoed? Is thy pedigree
>   As long, as wide as mine? For otherwise
>   Thou wert most unworthy; and 'twere loss of honour
>   In me to fight. More: I have drawn five teeth—
>   If thine stand sound, the terms are much unequal;
>   And, by strict laws of duel, I am excused
>   To fight on disadvantage."—
>   *Albumazar*, Act IV. Sec. 7.

In Beaumont and Fletcher's admirable play of *A King and no King*, there is some excellent mirth at the expense of the professors of the point of honour.

But though such shifts might occasionally be resorted to by the fainthearted, yet the fiery cavaliers of the English court were but little apt to profit by them; though their vengeance for insulted honour sometimes vented itself through fouler channels than that of fair combat. It happened, for example, that Lord Sanquhar, a Scottish nobleman, in fencing with a master of the noble science of defence, lost his eye by an unlucky thrust. The accident was provoking, but without remedy; nor did Lord Sanquhar think of it, unless with regret, until some years after, when he chanced to be in the French court. Henry the Great casually asked him, how he lost his eye? "By the thrust of a sword," answered Lord Sanquhar, not caring to enter into particulars. The king, supposing the accident the consequence of a duel, immediately enquired, " Does the man yet live?" These few words set the blood of the

Scottish nobleman on fire; nor did he rest till he had taken the base vengeance of assassinating, by hired ruffians, the unfortunate fencing-master. The mutual animosity, betwixt the English and Scottish nations, had already occasioned much bloodshed among the gentry by single combat, and James now found himself under the necessity of making a striking example of one of his Scottish nobles, to avoid the imputation of the grossest partiality. Lord Sanquhar was condemned to be hanged, and suffered that ignominious punishment accordingly.

By a circuitous route, we are now arrived at the subject of our ballad; for to the tragical duel of Stuart and Wharton, and to other instances of bloody combats and brawls betwixt the two nations, is imputed James's firmness in the case of Lord Sanquhar.

"For Ramsay, one of the king's servants, not long before Sanquhar's trial, had switched the Earl of Montgomery, who was the king's first favourite, happily because he took it so. Maxwell, another of them, had bitten Hawley, a gentleman of the Temple, by the ear, which enraged the Templars, (in those times riotous, subject to tumults,) and brought it almost to a national quarrel, till the king stopt it, and took it up himself. The Lord Bruce had summoned Sir Edward Sackville, (afterwards Earl of Dorset,) into France, with a fatal compliment to take death from his hand.[1] And the

---

[1] See an account of this desperate duel in the *Guardian*.

much-lamented Sir James Stuart, one of the King's blood, and Sir George Wharton, the prime branch of that noble family, for little worthless punctilios of honour, (being intimate friends,) took the field, and fell together by each other's hand."—Wilson's Life of James VI. p. 60.

The sufferers in this melancholy affair were both men of high birth, the heirs-apparent of two noble families, and youths of the most promising expectation. Sir James Stuart was a knight of the Bath, and eldest son of Walter, first Lord Blantyre, by Nicholas, daughter of Sir James Somerville of Cambusnethan. Sir George Wharton was also a knight of the Bath, and eldest son of Philip, Lord Wharton, by Frances, daughter of Henry Clifford, Earl of Cumberland. He married Anne, daughter of the Earl of Rutland, but left no issue.

The circumstances of the quarrel and combat are accurately detailed in the ballad, of which there exists a black-letter copy in the Pearson Collection, now in the library of John, Duke of Roxburghe, entitled, " A Lamentable Ballad, of a Combate, lately fought near London, between Sir James Stewarde, and Sir George Wharton, knights, who were both slain at that time.—To the tune of *Down Plimpton Park*," &c. A copy of this ballad has been published in Mr Ritson's *Ancient Songs*, and, upon comparison, appears very little different from that which has been preserved by tradition in Ettrick Forest. Two verses have been added, and one considerably improved, from Mr Ritson's edition. These three stanzas are the fifth and ninth of Part First, and the penult verse of Part Second. I am thus particular, that the reader may be able, if he pleases, to compare the traditional ballad with the original edition. It furnishes striking evidence, that "without characters, fame lives long." The difference, chiefly to be remarked betwixt the copies, lies in the dialect, and in some modifications applicable to Scotland; as, using the words " *Our Scottish Knight.*" The black-letter ballad, in like manner, terms Wharton " *Our English Knight.*"

My correspondent, James Hogg, adds the following note to this ballad:—" I have heard this song sung by several old people; but all of them with this tradition, that Wharton bribed Stuart's second, and actually fought in armour. I acknowledge, that, from some dark hints in the song, this appears not impossible; but that you may not judge too rashly, I must remind you, that the old people, inhabiting the head-lands (high ground) hereabouts, although possessed of many original songs, traditions, and anecdotes, are most unreasonably partial when the valour or honour of a Scotsman is called in question." I retain this note, because it is characteristic; but I agree with my correspondent, there can be no foundation for the tradition, except in national partiality.[1]

[1] Since the first publication of this work, I have seen cause to think that this insinuation was not introduced by Scottish reciters, but really founded upon the opinion formed by Stuart's friends. Sir

James Stuart married the Lady Dorothy Hastings; and, in a letter from the late venerable Countess of Moira and Hastings, he is described, from family tradition, as the most accomplished person of the age he lived in, and, in talents and abilities, almost equal to what is recorded of the Admirable Crichton. Sir George Wharton is, on the other hand, affirmed to have been a man of a fierce and brutal temper, and to have provoked the quarrel, by wanton and intolerable reflections on the Scottish national character. "In the duel," her ladyship concludes, "family tradition does not allow Sir James to have been killed fairly." From an anecdote respecting Sir George Wharton's conduct in a quarrel with the Earl of Pembroke, there is room to suppose the imputations on his temper were not without foundation. See LODGE's *Illustrations of English History*, vol. iii. p. 350. Lady Moira concludes, that she had seen a copy of the ballad different from any one hitherto printed, in which the charge of foul play was directly stated against Wharton.

THE
DUEL OF WHARTON AND STUART.

PART FIRST.

It grieveth me to tell you o'
    Near London late what did befall,
'Twixt two young gallant gentlemen;
    It grieveth me, and ever shall.

One of them was Sir George Wharton,
    My good Lord Wharton's son and heir;
The other, James Stuart, a Scottish knight,
    One that a valiant heart did bear.

When first to court these nobles came,
    One night, a-gaming, fell to words;[1]

---

[1] Sir George Wharton was quarrelsome at cards; a temper which he exhibited so disagreeably when playing with the Earl of Pembroke, that the Earl told him, "Sir George, I have loved you long; but, by your manner in playing, you lay it upon me either to leave to love you, or to leave to play with you; wherefore choosing to love you still, I will never play with you any more."—Lodge's *Illustrations*, vol. iii. p. 350.

And in their fury grew so hot,
  That they did both try their keen swords.

No manner of treating, nor advice,
  Could hold from striking in that place;
For, in the height and heat of blood,
  James struck George Wharton on the face.

" What doth this mean," George Wharton said,
  " To strike in such unmanly sort?
But, that I take it at thy hands,
  The tongue of man shall ne'er report!"—

" But do thy worst, then," said Sir James,
  " Now do thy worst, appoint a day!
There's not a lord in England breathes
  Shall gar me give an inch of way."—

" Ye brag right weel," George Wharton said;
  " Let our brave lords at large alane,
And speak of me, that am thy foe,
  For you shall find enough o' one!

" I'll interchange my glove wi' thine;
  I'll show it on the bed of death;
I mean the place where we shall fight;
  There ane or both maun lose life and breath!"—

" We'll meet near Waltham," said Sir James;
  " To-morrow, that shall be the day.

We'll either take a single man,
    And try who bears the bell away."

Then down together hands they shook,
    Without any envious sign;
Then went to Ludgate, where they lay,
    And each man drank his pint of wine.

No kind of envy could be seen,
    No kind of malice they did betray;
But a' was clear and calm as death,
    Whatever in their bosoms lay,

Till parting time; and then, indeed,
    They show'd some rancour in their heart;
"Next time we meet," says George Wharton,
    "Not half sae soundly we shall part!"

So they have parted, firmly bent
    Their valiant minds equal to try:
The second part shall clearly show,
    Both how they meet, and how they die.

THE
DUEL OF WHARTON AND STUART.

PART SECOND.

George Wharton was the first ae man,
  Came to the appointed place that day,
Where he espyed our Scots lord coming,
  As fast as he could post away.

They met, shook hands; their cheeks were pale;
  Then to George Wharton James did say,
" I dinna like your doublet, George,
  It stands sae weel on you this day.

" Say, have you got no armour on ?
  Have you no under robe of steel ?
I never saw an Englishman
  Become his doublet half sae weel."—

" Fy no! fy no!" George Wharton said,
  " For that's the thing that mauna be,

That I should come wi' armour on,
    And you a naked man truly."—

" Our men shall search our doublets, George,
    And see if one of us do lie;
Then will we prove, wi' weapons sharp,
    Ourselves true gallants for to be."—

Then they threw off their doublets both,
    And stood up in their sarks of lawn;
" Now, take my counsel," said Sir James,
    " Wharton, to thee I'll make it known:

" So as we stand, so will we fight;
    Thus naked in our sarks," said he;
" Fy no! fy no!" George Wharton says,
    " That is the thing that must not be.

" We're neither drinkers, quarrellers,
    Nor men that cares na for oursell,
Nor minds na what we're gaun about,
    Or if we're gaun to heav'n or hell.

" Let us to God bequeath our souls,
    Our bodies to the dust and clay!"
With that he drew his deadly sword,
    The first was drawn on field that day.

Se'en bouts and turns these heroes had,
    Or e'er a drop o' blood was drawn;

Our Scotch lord, wond'ring, quickly cry'd,
   "Stout Wharton! thou still hauds thy awn!"—

The first stroke that George Wharton gae,
   He struck him thro' the shoulder-bane;
The neist was thro' the thick o' the thigh;
   He thought our Scotch lord had been slain.

"Oh! ever alack!" George Wharton cry'd,
   "Art thou a living man, tell me?
If there's a surgeon living can,
   He's cure thy wounds right speedily."—

"No more of that," James Stuart said;
   "Speak not of curing wounds to me!
For one of us must yield our breath,
   Ere off the field one foot we flee."—

They looked oure their shoulders both,
   To see what company was there:
They both had grievous marks of death,
   But frae the other nane wad steer.

George Wharton was the first that fell;
   Our Scotch lord fell immediately:
They both did cry to Him above,
   To save their souls, for they boud die.

THE LAMENT

OF

THE BORDER WIDOW.

This fragment, obtained from recitation in the Forest of Ettrick, is said to relate to the execution of Cockburne of Henderland, a Border freebooter, hanged over the gate of his own tower, by James V., in the course of that memorable expedition, in 1529, which was fatal to Johnie Armstrong, Adam Scott of Tushielaw, and many other marauders. The vestiges of the castle of Henderland are still to be traced upon the farm of that name, belonging to Mr Murray of Henderland. They are situated near the mouth of the river Meggat, which falls into the lake of St Mary, in Selkirkshire. The adjacent country, which now hardly bears a single tree, is celebrated by Lesly, as, in his time, affording shelter to the largest stags in Scotland. A mountain torrent, called Henderland Burn, rushes impetuously from the hills, through a rocky chasm, named the Dowglen, and passes near the site of the tower. To the

recesses of this glen, the wife of Cockburne is said to
have retreated, during the execution of her husband;
and a place, called the *Lady's Seat*, is still shown,
where she is said to have striven to drown, amid the
roar of a foaming cataract, the tumultuous noise, which
announced the close of his existence. In a deserted
burial-place, which once surrounded the chapel of the
castle, the monument of Cockburne and his lady is still
shown. It is a large stone, broken in three parts; but
some armorial bearings may yet be traced, and the following inscription is still legible, though defaced:—

>   HERE LYES PERYS OF COKBURNE AND HIS
>   WYFE MARJORY.

Tradition says, that Cockburne was surprised by the
king, while sitting at dinner. After the execution,
James marched rapidly forward, to surprise Adam Scott
of Tushielaw, called the King of the Border, and sometimes the King of Thieves. A path through the mountains, which separate the vale of Ettrick from the head
of Yarrow, is still called the *King's Road*, and seems
to have been the route which he followed. The remains
of the tower of Tushielaw are yet visible, overhanging
the wild banks of the Ettrick; and are an object of
terror to the benighted peasant, from an idea of their
being haunted by spectres. From these heights, and
through the adjacent county of Peebles, passes a wild
path, called still the *Thief's Road*, from having been
used chiefly by the marauders of the Border.

THE LAMENT

OF

THE BORDER WIDOW.

My love he built me a bonny bower,
And clad it a' wi' lilye flour,
A brawer bower ye ne'er did see,
Than my true love he built for me.

There came a man, by middle day,
He spied his sport, and went away;
And brought the King that very night,
Who brake my bower, and slew my knight.

He slew my knight, to me sae dear;
He slew my knight, and poin'd[1] his gear;
My servants all for life did flee,
And left me in extremitie.

I sew'd his sheet, making my mane;
I watch'd the corpse, myself alane;

[1] *Poin'd*—Poinded, attached by legal distress.

I watch'd his body, night and day ;
No living creature came that way.

I took his body on my back,
And whiles I gaed, and whiles I sat ;
I digg'd a grave, and laid him in,
And happ'd him with the sod sae green.

But think na ye my heart was sair,
When I laid the moul' on his yellow hair ;
O think na ye my heart was wae,
When I turn'd about, away to gae ?

Nae living man I'll love again,
Since that my lovely knight is slain ;
Wi' ae lock of his yellow hair
I'll chain my heart for evermair.

FAIR HELEN OF KIRCONNELL.

The following very popular ballad has been handed down by tradition in its present imperfect state. The affecting incident, on which it is founded, is well known. A lady, of the name of Helen Irving, or Bell,[1] (for this is disputed by the two clans,) daughter of the Laird of Kirconnell, in Dumfries-shire, and celebrated for her beauty, was beloved by two gentlemen in the neighbourhood. The name of the favoured suitor was Adam Fleming of Kirkpatrick; that of the other has escaped tradition: though it has been alleged, that he was a Bell, of Blacket House. The addresses of the latter were, however, favoured by the friends of the lady, and the lovers were therefore obliged to meet in secret, and by night, in the churchyard of Kirconnell, a romantic

---

[1] This dispute is owing to the uncertain date of the ballad; for, although the last proprietors of Kirconnell were Irvings, when deprived of their possessions by Robert Maxwell in 1600, yet Kirconnell is termed in old chronicles, *The Bell's Tower;* and a stone, with the arms of that family, has been found among its ruins. Fair Helen's sirname, therefore, depends upon the period at which she lived, which it is now impossible to ascertain.

spot, almost surrounded by the river Kirtle. During one of these private interviews, the jealous and despised lover suddenly appeared on the opposite bank of the stream, and levelled his carabine at the breast of his rival. Helen threw herself before her lover, received in her bosom the bullet, and died in his arms. A desperate and mortal combat ensued between Fleming and the murderer, in which the latter was cut to pieces. Other accounts say, that Fleming pursued his enemy to Spain, and slew him in the streets of Madrid.

The ballad, as now published, consists of two parts. The first seems to be an address, either by Fleming or his rival, to the lady; if, indeed, it constituted any portion of the original poem. For the Editor cannot help suspecting, that these verses have been the production of a different and inferior bard, and only adapted to the original measure and tune. But this suspicion being unwarranted by any copy he has been able to procure, he does not venture to do more than intimate his own opinion. The second part, by far the most beautiful, and which is unquestionably original, forms the lament of Fleming over the grave of fair Helen.

The ballad is here given, without alteration or improvement, from the most accurate copy which could be recovered. The fate of Helen has not, however, remained unsung by modern bards. A lament, of great poetical merit, by the learned historian, Mr Pinkerton, with several other poems on this subject, have been printed in various forms.

The grave of the lovers is yet shown in the churchyard of Kirconnell, near Springkell. Upon the tombstone can still be read—*Hic jacet Adamus Fleming;* a cross and sword are sculptured on the stone. The former is called by the country people, the gun with which Helen was murdered; and the latter, the avenging sword of her lover. *Sit illis terra levis!* A heap of stones is raised on the spot where the murder was committed; a token of abhorrence common to most nations.[1]

[1] This practice has only very lately become obsolete in Scotland. But a few years ago, a cairn was pointed out to me in the King's Park of Edinburgh, which had been raised in detestation of a cruel murder, perpetrated by one Nicol Muschat, on the body of his wife, in that place, in the year 1720. [This is the *Muschat's Cairn* of the Heart of Mid-Lothian.—ED.]

FAIR HELEN.

PART FIRST.

O! sweetest sweet, and fairest fair,
Of birth and worth beyond compare,
Thou art the causer of my care,
   Since first I loved thee.

Yet God hath given to me a mind,
The which to thee shall prove as kind
As any one that thou shalt find,
   Of high or low degree.

The shallowest water makes maist din,
The deadest pool, the deepest linn;
The richest man least truth within,
   Though he preferred be.

Yet, nevertheless, I am content,
And never a whit my love repent,
But think the time was a' weel spent,
   Though I disdained be.

O! Helen sweet, and maist complete,
My captive spirit's at thy feet!
Thinks thou still fit thus for to treat
  Thy captive cruelly?

O! Helen brave! but this I crave,
Of thy poor slave some pity have,
And do him save that's near his grave,
  And dies for love of thee.

FAIR HELEN.

PART SECOND.

I wish I were where Helen lies,
Night and day on me she cries;
O that I were where Helen lies,
   On fair Kirconnell Lee!

Curst be the heart that thought the thought,
And curst the hand that fired the shot,
When in my arms burd [1] Helen dropt,
   And died to succour me!

O think na ye my heart was sair,
When my love dropt down and spak nae mair!
There did she swoon wi' meikle care,
   On fair Kirconnell Lee.

As I went down the water side,
None but my foe to be my guide,

[1] *Burd Helen*—Maid Helen.

None but my foe to be my guide,
   On fair Kirconnell Lee;

I lighted down my sword to draw,
I hacked him in pieces sma',
I hacked him in pieces sma',
   For her sake that died for me.

O Helen fair, beyond compare!..
I'll make a garland of thy hair,
Shall bind my heart for evermair,
   Until the day I die.

O that I were where Helen lies!
Night and day on me she cries;
Out of my bed she bids me rise,
   Says, "Haste and come to me!"—

O Helen fair! O Helen chaste!
If I were with thee, I were blest,
Where thou lies low, and takes thy rest,
   On fair Kirconnell Lee.

I wish my grave were growing green,
A winding-sheet drawn ower my een,
And I in Helen's arms lying,
   On fair Kirconnell Lee.

I wish I were where Helen lies!
Night and day on me she cries;

And I am weary of the skies,
 For her sake that died for me.[1]

[1] [The Edinburgh Reviewer for January, 1803, quotes verses 1—8 of the 2d part of this ballad, as "of exquisite merit." The fate of Fair Helen has since been celebrated by Wordsworth, in these beautiful stanzas:—

"Fair Ellen Irwin, when she sat
 Upon the Braes of Kirtle,
Was lovely as a Grecian Maid,
 Adorned with wreaths of myrtle.
Young Adam Bruce beside her lay;
And there did they beguile the day
With love and gentle speeches,
Beneath the budding beeches.

"From many Knights and many Squires
 The Bruce had been selected;
And Gordon, fairest of them all,
 By Ellen was rejected.
Sad tidings to that noble youth!
For it may be proclaimed with truth,
If Bruce hath loved sincerely,
That Gordon loves as dearly.

"But what is Gordon's beauteous face?
 And what are Gordon's crosses,
To them who sit by Kirtle's braes,
 Upon the verdant mosses?
Alas that ever he was born!
The Gordon, couched behind a thorn,
Sees them and their caressing,
Beholds them blest and blessing.

"Proud Gordon cannot hear the thoughts
 That through his brain are travelling,—
And starting up, to Bruce's heart
 He launched a deadly javelin!
Fair Ellen saw it when it came,
And, stepping forth to meet the same,

Did with her body cover
The youth, her chosen lover.

"And, falling into Bruce's arms,
　Thus died the beauteous Ellen,
Thus from the heart of her true-love,
　The mortal spear repelling.
And Bruce, as soon as he had slain
The Gordon, sailed away to Spain;
And fought with rage incessant
Against the Moorish Crescent.

"But many days, and many months,
　And many years ensuing,
This wretched Knight did vainly seek
　The death that he was wooing:
And coming back across the wave,
Without a groan on Helen's grave
His body he extended,
And there his sorrow ended.

"Now ye, who willingly have heard
　The tale I have been telling,
May in Kirkonnell churchyard view
　The grave of lovely Ellen:
By Ellen's side the Bruce is laid;
And, for the stone upon his head,
May no rude hand deface it,
And its forlorn Hic Jacet!"]

HUGHIE THE GRÆME.

The Græmes, as we have had frequent occasion to notice, were a powerful and numerous clan, who chiefly inhabited the Debateable Land. They were said to be of Scottish extraction; and their chief claimed his descent from Malice, Earl of Stratherne. In military service they were more attached to England than to Scotland; but in their depredations on both countries, they appear to have been very impartial; for, in the year 1600, the gentlemen of Cumberland alleged to Lord Scroope, "that the Græmes, and their clans, with their children, tenants, and servants, were the chiefest actors in the spoil and decay of the country." Accordingly, they were, at that time, obliged to give a bond of surety for each other's peaceable demeanour; from which bond, their numbers appear to have exceeded four hundred men.—*See Introduction to* Nicolson's *History of Cumberland,* p. cviii.

Richard Græme, of the family of Netherby, was one of the attendants upon Charles I., when Prince of Wales, and accompanied him upon his romantic journey through France and Spain. The following little anecdote, which then occurred, will show that the memory of the Græmes' Border exploits was at that time still preserved.

"They were now entered into the deep time of Lent, and could get no flesh in their inns. Whereupon fell out a pleasant passage, if I may insert it, by the way, among more serious. There was, near Bayonne, a herd of goats, with their young ones; upon the sight whereof, Sir Richard Graham tells the Marquis (of Buckingham), that he would snap one of the kids, and make some shift to carry him snug to their lodging. Which the Prince overhearing, 'Why, Richard,' says he, 'do you think you may practise here your old tricks upon the Borders?' Upon which words, they, in the first place, gave the goat-herd good contentment: and then, while the Marquis and Richard, being both on foot, were chasing the kid about the stack, the Prince, from horseback, killed him in the head, with a Scottish pistol.—Which circumstance, though trifling, may yet serve to show how his loyal Highness, even in such slight and sportful damage, had a noble sense of just dealing."—*Sir* H. Wotton's *Life of the Duke of Buckingham.*

I find no traces of this particular Hughie Græme, of the ballad; but, from the mention of the *Bishop*, I suspect he may have been one of about four hundred Borderers, against whom bills of complaint were exhibited to Robert Aldridge, Lord Bishop of Carlisle, about 1553, for divers incursions, burnings, murders,

mutilations, and spoils, by them committed.—NICOL-
SON's *History, Introduction*, lxxxi. There appear a
number of Græmes, in the specimen which we have of
that list of delinquents. There occur, in particular,

        Ritchie Grame of Bailie,
        Will's Jock Grame,
        Fargue's Willie Grame,
        Muckle Willie Grame,
        Will Grame of Rosetrees,
        Ritchie Grame, younger of Netherby,
        Wat Grame, called Flaughtail,
        Will Grame, Nimble Willie,
        Will Grame, Mickle Willie,

with many others.

In Mr Ritson's curious and valuable collection of legendary poetry, entitled *Ancient Songs*, he has published this Border ditty, from a collation of two old black-letter copies, one in the collection of the late John, Duke of Roxburghe, and another in the hands of John Bayne, Esq.—The learned Editor mentions another copy, beginning, "Good Lord John is a hunting gone." The present edition was procured for me by my friend Mr William Laidlaw, in Blackhouse, and has been long current in Selkirkshire; but Mr Ritson's copy has occasionally been resorted to for better readings.

HUGHIE THE GRÆME.

Gude Lord Scroope's to the hunting gane,
    He has ridden o'er moss and muir;
And he has grippit Hughie the Græme,
    For stealing o' the Bishop's mare.

"Now, good Lord Scroope, this may not be!
    Here hangs a broadsword by my side;
And if that thou canst conquer me,
    The matter it may soon be tryed."—

"I ne'er was afraid of a traitor thief;
    Although thy name be Hughie the Græme,
I'll make thee repent thee of thy deeds,
    If God but grant me life and time."—

"Then do your worst now, good Lord Scroope,
    And deal your blows as hard as you can!
It shall be tried within an hour,
    Which of us two is the better man."—

But as they were dealing their blows so free,
    And both so bloody at the time,

Over the moss came ten yeomen so tall,
    All for to take brave Hughie the Græme.

Then they hae grippit Hughie the Græme,
    And brought him up through Carlisle town;
The lasses and lads stood on the walls,
    Crying, " Hughie the Græme, thou'se ne'er gae down!"—

Then they hae chosen a jury of men,
    The best that were in Carlisle[1] town;
And twelve of them cried out at once,
    " Hughie the Græme, thou must gae down!"—

Then up bespak him gude Lord Hume,[2]
    As he sat by the judge's knee,—
" Twenty white owsen, my gude lord,
    If you'll grant Hughie the Græme to me."—

" O no, O no, my gude Lord Hume!
    For sooth and sae it mauna be;
For, were there but three Græmes of the name,
    They suld be hanged a' for me."—

'Twas up and spake the gude Lady Hume,
    As she sat by the judge's knee,—
" A peck of white pennies, my gude lord judge,
    If you'll grant Hughie the Græme to me."

[1] *Garland*—Anc. Songs.—[2] *Doles*—Anc. Songs.

"O no, O no, my gude Lady Hume!
  Forsooth and so it must na be;
Were he but the one Græme of the name,
  He suld be hanged high for me."—

"If I be guilty," said Hughie the Græme,
  "Of me my friends shall have small talk;"
And he has louped fifteen feet and three,
  Though his hands they were tied behind his back.

He looked over his left shoulder,
  And for to see what he might see;
There was he aware of his auld father,
  Came tearing his hair most piteouslie.

"O hald your tongue, my father," he says,
  "And see that ye dinna weep for me!
For they may ravish me o' my life,
  But they canna banish me fro' Heaven hie.

"Fair ye weel, fair Maggie, my wife!
  The last time we came ower the muir,
'Twas thou bereft me of my life,
  And wi' the Bishop thou play'd the whore.'

---

[1] Of the morality of Robert Aldridge, Bishop of Carlisle, we know but little; but his political and religious faith were of a stretching and accommodating texture. Anthony a Wood observes, that there were many changes in his time, both in church and state; but that the worthy prelate retained his offices and preferments during them all.

"Here, Johnie Armstrang, take thou my sword,
 That is made o' the metal sae fine;
And when thou comest to the English[1] side,
 Remember the death of Hughie the Græme."

[1] *Border*—Anc. Songs.

JOHNIE OF BREADISLEE.

AN ANCIENT NITHSDALE BALLAD.

The hero of this ballad appears to have been an outlaw and deer-stealer—probably one of the broken men residing upon the Border. There are several different copies, in one of which the principal personage is called *Johnie of Cockielaw*. The stanzas of greatest merit have been selected from each copy. It is sometimes said, that this outlaw possessed the old Castle of Morton, in Dumfries-shire, now ruinous:—" Near to this castle there was a park, built by Sir Thomas Randolph, on the face of a very great and high hill; so artificially, that, by the advantage of the hill, all wild beasts, such as deers, harts, and roes, and hares, did easily leap in, but could not get out again; and if any other cattle, such as cows, sheep, or goats, did voluntarily leap in, or were forced to do it, *it is doubted* if their owners were permitted to get them out again." *Account of Presbytery of Penpont, apud Macfarlane's MSS.* Such a park would form a convenient domain to an outlaw's castle, and the mention of Durrisdeer, a neighbouring parish, adds weight to the tradition. I have seen on a mountain near Callendar, a sort of pinfold, composed of immense rocks, piled upon each other, which, I was told, was anciently constructed for the above-mentioned purpose. The mountain is thence called *Uah var*, or the *Cove of the Giant*.

JOHNIE OF BREADISLEE.

Johnie rose up in a May morning,
    Call'd for water to wash his hands—
"Gar loose to me the gude graie dogs,
    That are bound wi' iron bands."—

When Johnie's mother gat word o' that,
    Her hands for dule she wrang—
"O Johnie! for my benison,
    To the greenwood dinna gang!

"Eneugh ye hae o' gude wheat bread,
    And eneugh o' the blood-red wine;
And, therefore, for nae venison, Johnie,
    I pray ye, stir frae hame."—

But Johnie's busk't up his gude bend bow,
    His arrows, ane by ane;
And he has gane to Durrisdeer,
    To hunt the dun deer down.

As he came down by Merriemass,
    And in by the benty line,

There has he espied a deer lying
  Aneath a bush of ling.¹

Johnie he shot, and the dun deer lap,
  And he wounded her on the side;
But, atween the water and the brae,
  His hounds they laid her pride.

And Johnie has bryttled² the deer sae weel,
  That he's had out her liver and lungs;
And wi' these he has feasted his bluidy hounds,
  As if they had been earl's sons.

They eat sae much o' the venison,
  And drank sae much o' the blude,
That Johnie and a' his bluidy hounds,
  Fell asleep as they had been dead.

And by there came a silly auld carle,
  An ill death mote he die!
For he's awa' to Hislinton,
  Where the Seven Foresters did lie.

" What news, what news, ye gray-headed carle,
  What news bring ye to me?"—
" I bring nae news," said the gray-headed carle,
  " Save what these eyes did see.

¹ *Ling*—Heath.—² *Bryttle*—To cut up venison. See the Ancient ballad of *Chevy Chace*, v. 8.

"As I came down by Merriemass,
   And down among the scroggs,[1]
The bonniest childe that ever I saw
   Lay sleeping amang his dogs.

"The shirt that was upon his back
   Was o' the Holland fine;
The doublet which was over that
   Was o' the lincome twine.[2]

"The buttons that were on his sleeve
   Were o' the goud sae gude:
The gude graie hounds he lay amang,
   Their mouths were dyed wi' blude."—

Then out and spak the First Forester,
   The heid man ower them a'—
"If this be Johnie o' Breadislee,
   Nae nearer will we draw."—

But up and spak the Sixth Forester,
   (His sister's son was he,)
"If this be Johnie o' Breadislee,
   We soon shall gar him die!"—

The first flight of arrows the Foresters shot,
   They wounded him on the knee;

---

[1] *Scroggs*—Stunted trees.—[2] The Lincoln manufacture.

And out and spak the Seventh Forester,
  "The next will gar him die."

Johnie's set his back against an aik,
  His fute against a stane;
And he has slain the Seven Foresters,
  He has slain them a' but ane.

He has broke three ribs in that ane's side;
  But and his collar bane;
He's laid him twa-fald ower his steed,
  Bade him carry the tidings hame.

"O is there nae a bonnie bird,
  Can sing as I can say;
Could flee away to my mother's bower,
  And tell to fetch Johnie away?"—[1]

The starling flew to his mother's window stane,
  It whistled and it sang;
And aye the ower word o' the tune
  Was—"Johnie tarries lang!"

[1] [Perhaps here should be inserted the beautiful stanza preserved by Finlay, so descriptive, as he remarks, of the languor of death:

    "There's no a bird in a' this forest
    Will do as meikle for me,
    As dip its wing in the wan water,
    And straik it on my ee-bree."
                    MOTHERWELL, p. 22.]

They made a rod o' the hazel bush,
    Another o' the slae-thorn tree,
And mony mony were the men
    At fetching o'er Johnie.

Then out and spak his auld mother,
    And fast her tears did fa'—
" Ye wad nae be warn'd, my son Johnie,
    Frae the hunting to bide awa'.

" Aft hae I brought to Breadislee,
    The less gear[1] and the mair,
But I ne'er brought to Breadislee,
    What grieved my heart sae sair.

" But wae betyde that silly auld carle!
    An ill death shall he die!
For the highest tree in Merriemas
    Shall be his morning's fee."

Now Johnie's gude bend bow is broke,
    And his gude graie dogs are slain;
And his bodie lies dead in Durrisdeer,
    And his hunting it is done.[2]

---

[1] *Gear*—Usually signifies *goods*, but here *spoil*.

[2] [Mr Motherwell has printed some stanzas of perhaps a more ancient set of this ballad—*e. g.*

    V. 2.—" Johnie lookit east, and Johnie lookit west,
        And it's lang before the sun, sun;

And there did he spy the dun deer lie
Beneath a bush o' brume, brume,
Beneath a bush o' brume."

V. 5.—" It's down, and it's down, and it's down, down,
And it's down among the scrogs, scrogs;
And it's there ye'll espy twa bonny boys lie
Asleep amang their dogs, dogs,
Asleep amang their dogs."—P. 23.]

KATHARINE JANFARIE.

The Ballad was published in the first edition of this work, under the title of "The Laird of Laminton." It is now given in a more perfect state, from several recited copies. The residence of the lady, and the scene of the affray at her bridal, is said, by old people, to have been upon the banks of the Cadden, near to where it joins the Tweed.—Others say the skirmish was fought near Traquair, and KATHARINE JANFARIE'S *dwelling was in the glen about three miles above Traquair House.*[1]

There was a may, and a weel-far'd may,
    Lived high up in yon glen:
Her name was Katharine Janfarie,
    She was courted by mony men.

Up then came Lord Lauderdale,
    Up frae the Lawland Border;

---

[1] [At page 225 of Motherwell, the reader will find another version of this ballad, in which the heroine bears not the name of *Janfarie* but *Johnstone*, and her lover is, as in the first edition of the Minstrelsy, the Laird of Lamington—*i. e.* Baillie of Lammington, in Clydesdale, the head of that ancient name.—ED.]

And he has come to court this may,
    A' mounted in good order.

He told na her father, he told na her mother,
    And he told na ane o' her kin;
But he whisper'd the bonnie lassie hersell,
    And has her favour won.

But out then cam Lord Lochinvar,[1]
    Out frae the English Border,
All for to court this bonny may,
    Weel mounted, and in order.

He told her father, he told her mother,
    And a' the lave o' her kin;
But he told na the bonnie may hersell,
    Till on her wedding e'en.

She sent to the Lord o' Lauderdale,
    Gin he wad come and see;
And he has sent word back again,
    Weel answer'd she suld be.

And he has sent a messenger
    Right quickly through the land,
And raised mony an armed man
    To be at his command.

---

[1] [Gordon of Lochinvar, head of a powerful branch of that name, afterwards Viscounts of Lochinvar.]

The bride looked out at a high window,
    Beheld baith dale and down,
And she was aware of her first true love,
    With riders mony a one.

She scoffed him, and scorned him,
    Upon her wedding day;
And said—" It was the Fairy court
    To see him in array!

" O come ye here to fight, young lord,
    Or come ye here to play?
Or come ye here to drink good wine
    Upon the wedding day?"—[1]

" I come na here to fight," he said,
    " I come na here to play;
I'll but lead a dance wi' the bonny bride,
    And mount, and go my way."[2]

It is a glass of the blood-red wine
    Was filled up them between,

---

[1] ["Then spoke the bride's father, his hand on his sword,
(For the poor craven bridegroom said never a word,)
' O come ye in peace here, or come ye in war,
Or to dance at our bridal, young Lord Lochinvar?'"
    Lady Heron's Songs. Marmion, Canto V.]

[2] [" ' I long woo'd your daughter, my suit ye denied;—
Love swells like the Solway, but ebbs like its tide—
And now am I come, with this lost love of mine,
To lead but one measure, drink one cup of wine '"
    Ibid.]

And aye she drank to Lauderdale,
  Wha her true love had been.[1]

He's ta'en her by the milk-white hand,
  And by the grass-green sleeve;
He's mounted her hie behind himsell,
  At her kinsmen speir'd na leave.[2]

" Now take your bride, Lord Lochinvar!
  Now take her if you may!
But, if you take your bride again,
  We'll call it but foul play."

There were four-and-twenty bonnie boys,
  A' clad in the Johnstone grey;[3]

---

[1] [" The bride kiss'd the goblet; the knight took it up,
He quaffed off the wine, and he threw down the cup.
She looked down to blush, and she looked up to sigh,
With a smile on her lips, and a tear in her eye."
          Lady Heron's Song. Marmion, Canto V.]

[2] [" One touch to her hand, and one word in her ear,
When they reach'd the hall door, and the charger stood near;
So light to the croupe the fair lady he swung,
So light to the saddle before her he sprung!
' She is won! we are gone, over bank, bush, and scaur;
They'll have fleet steeds that follow,' quoth young Lochinvar."
          Ibid.]

[3] *Johnstone Grey*—The livery of the ancient family of Johnstone. [This circumstance appears to support the Clydesdale copy, which gives Katharine the surname of Johnstone. I incline to suspect that she was a Johnstone of *Wamphray,* and that Katharine o' Wamphray had been blundered, by the Ettrick reciters, into Katharine Jeffrey, vulgarly pronounced *Janfray.*—ED.]

They said they would take the bride again,
　　By the strong hand, if they may.

Some o' them were right willing men,
　　But they were na willing a';
And four-and-twenty Leader lads
　　Bid them mount and ride awa'.

Then whingers flew frae gentles' sides,
　　And swords flew frae the shea's,
And red and rosy was the blood
　　Ran down the lily braes.

The blood ran down by Caddon bank,
　　And down by Caddon brae;
And, sighing, said the bonnie bride—
　　" O wae's me for foul play!"[1]

My blessing on your heart, sweet thing!
　　Wae to your wilfu' will!
There's mony a gallant gentleman
　　Whae's bluid ye have garr'd to spill.

[1] [" It's up the Cowden bank,
　　And down the Cowden brae:
And aye she made the trumpet sound
　　It's a weel won play.
O meikle was the blood was shed
　　Upon the Cowden brae,
And aye she made the trumpet sound,
　　It's a' fair play."
　　　　　　　　　MOTHERWELL, p. 229.]

Now a' you lords of fair England,
   And that dwell by the English Border,
Come never here to seek a wife,
   For fear of sic disorder.

They'll haik ye up, and settle ye bye,
   Till on your wedding day;
Then gie ye frogs instead of fish,
   And play ye foul foul play.

THE LAIRD O' LOGIE.

An edition of this ballad is current, under the title of " The Laird of Ochiltree;" but the Editor, since the first publication of this work, has been fortunate enough to recover the following more correct and ancient copy, as recited by a gentleman residing near Biggar. It agrees more nearly, both in the name and in the circumstances, with the real fact, than the printed ballad of Ochiltree.

In the year 1592, Francis Stuart, Earl of Bothwell, was agitating his frantic and ill-concerted attempts against the person of James VI., whom he endeavoured to surprise in the Palace of Falkland. Through the emulation and private rancour of the courtiers, he found adherents even about the King's person; among whom, it seems, was the hero of our ballad, whose history is thus narrated in that curious and valuable chronicle, of which the first part has been published under the title of " The Historie of King James the Sext."

" In this close tyme it fortunit, that a gentleman, callit Weymis of Logye, being also in credence at court, was delatit as a traffekker with Frances Erle Bothwell;

and he, being examinat before King and counsall, confessit his accusation to be of veritie, that sundry tymes he had spokin with him, expresslie aganis the King's inhibitioun proclamit in the contrare, whilk confession he subscryvit with his hand; and because the event of this mater had sik a success, it sall also be praysit be my pen, as a worthie turne, proceiding from honest cheat love and charitie, whilk suld on na wayis be obscurit from the posteritie, for the gude example; and therefore I have thought gude to insert the same for a perpetual memorie.

"Queen Anne, our noble princess, was servit with dyverss gentilwemen of hir awin cuntrie, and naymelie with ane callit Mres Margaret Twynstoun,[1] to whome this gentilman, Weymes of Logye, bure great honest affection, tending to the godlie band of marriage, the whilk was honestlie requytet be the said gentilwoman, yea even in his greatest mister;[2] for howsone she understude the said gentilman to be in distress, and apperantlie be his confession to be puneist to the death, and she having prevelege to ly in the Queynis chalmer that same verie night of his accusation, whare the King was also reposing that same night, she came furth of the dure prevelie, bayth the prencis being then at quyet rest, and past to the chalmer, whare the said gentilman was put in custodie to certayne of the garde, and commandit thayme that immediatelie he sould be broght to

---

[1] Twynlace, according to Spottiswoode.—[2] Mister—necessity.

the King and Queyne, whareunto they geving sure credence, obeyit. But howsone she was cum bak to the chalmer dur, she desyrit the watches to stay till he sould cum furth agayne, and so she closit the dur, and convoyit the gentilman to a windo', whare she ministrat a long corde unto him to convoy himself doun upon; and sa, be hir gude cheritable help, he happelie escapit be the subteltie of love."

THE LAIRD O' LOGIE.

I will sing, if ye will hearken,
   If ye will hearken unto me;
The King has ta'en a poor prisoner,
   The wanton laird o' young Logie.

Young Logie's laid in Edinburgh chapel;
   Carmichael's the keeper o' the key;[1]
And may Margaret's lamenting sair,
   A' for the love of young Logie.[2]

" Lament, lament na, may Margaret,
   And of your weeping let me be;

---

[1] Sir John Carmichael of Carmichael, the hero of the ballad called the *Raid of the Reidswire*, was appointed captain of the king's guard in 1588, and usually had the keeping of state criminals of rank:

[2] [After stanza 2d, Mr Motherwell inserts, from recitation, the following:

    " May Margaret sits in the Queen's bowir
    Kincking her fingers ane by ane;
    Cursing the day that she erewas born,
    Or that ere she heard o' Logie's name."—P. 56.—Ed.]

For ye maun to the King himsell,
   To seek the life of young Logie."

May Margaret has kilted her green cleiding,
   And she has curl'd back her yellow hair—
" If I canna get young Logie's life,
   Farewell to Scotland for evermair."—

When she came before the King,
   She knelit lowly on her knee—
" O what's the matter, may Margaret?
   And what needs a' this courtesie?"—

" A boon, a boon, my noble liege,
   A boon, a boon, I beg o' thee!
And the first boon that I come to crave,
   Is to grant me the life of young Logie."—

" O na, O na, may Margaret,
   Forsooth, and so it manna be;
For a' the gowd o' fair Scotland
   Shall not save the life of young Logie."

But she has stown the King's redding kaim,[1]
   Likewise the Queen her wedding knife,
And sent the tokens to Carmichael,
   To cause young Logie get his life.

---

[1] *Redding kaim*—Comb for the hair.

She sent him a purse o' the red gowd,
    Another o' the white monie;
She sent him a pistol for each hand,
    And bade him shoot when he gat free.

When he came to the tolbooth stair,
    There he let his volley flee:
It made the King in his chamber start,
    E'en in the bed where he might be.

" Gae out, gae out, my merrymen a',
    And bid Carmichael come speak to me;
For I'll lay my life the pledge o' that,
    That yon's the shot o' young Logie."—

When Carmichael came before the King,
    He fell low down upon his knee:
The very first word that the King spake,
    Was—" Where's the laird of young Logie?"—

Carmichael turn'd him round about,
    (I wot the tear blinded his ee,)
" There came a token frae your grace,
    Has ta'en away the laird frae me."—

" Hast thou play'd me that, Carmichael?
    And hast thou play'd me that?" quoth he;
" The morn the justice court's to stand,
    And Logie's place ye maun supplie."

Carmichael's awa to Margaret's bower,
   Even as fast as he may dree—
"O if young Logie be within,
   Tell him to come and speak with me!"—

May Margaret turn'd her round about,
   (I wot a loud laugh laughed she,)
"The egg is chipp'd, the bird is flown,
   Ye'll see nae mair of young Logie."

The tane is shipped at the pier of Leith,
   The tother at the Queen's Ferrie:
And she's gotten a father to her bairn,
   The wanton laird of young Logie.

A LYKE-WAKE DIRGE.

This is a sort of charm sung by the lower ranks of Roman Catholics in some parts of the north of England, while watching a dead body, previous to interment. The tune is doleful and monotonous, and, joined to the mysterious import of the words, has a solemn effect. The word *sleet*, in the chorus, seems to be corrupted from *selt*, or salt; a quantity of which, in compliance with a popular superstition, is frequently placed on the breast of a corpse.

The late Mr Ritson found an illustration of this dirge in a MS. of the Cotton Library, containing an account of Cleveland, in Yorkshire, in the reign of Queen Elizabeth. It was kindly communicated to the Editor by Mr Frank, Mr Ritson's executor, and runs thus:—" When any dieth, certaine women sing a song to the dead bodie, recyting the journey that the partye deceased must goe; and they are of beliefe (such is their fondnesse) that once in their lives, it is good to give a pair of new shoes to a poor man, for as much as, after this life, they are to pass barefoote through a great launde, full of thornes and furzen, except by the meryte of the almes aforesaid they have redemed the forfeyte; for, at the edge of the launde, an oulde man shall meet them with the same shoes that were given by the partie when he was lyving; and, after he hath shodde them, dismisseth them to go through thick and thin, without scratch or scalle."—*Julius*, F. VI. 459.

The mythologic ideas of the dirge are common to various creeds. The Mahometan believes, that, in advancing to the final judgment-seat, he must traverse a bar of red-hot iron, stretched across a bottomless gulf. The good works of each true believer, assuming a substantial form, will then interpose betwixt his feet and this "*Bridge of Dread;*" but the wicked, having no such protection, must fall headlong into the abyss. —D'HERBELOT, *Bibliotheque Orientale.*

Passages, similar to this dirge, are also to be found in *Lady Culross's Dream*, as quoted in the second Dissertation prefixed by Mr Pinkerton to his *Select Scottish Ballads*, 2 vols. The dreamer journeys towards heaven, accompanied and assisted by a celestial guide:—

"Through dreadful dens, which made my heart aghast,
He bare me up when I began to tire.
Sometimes we clamb o'er craggy mountains high,
And sometimes stay'd on ugly braes of sand;
They were so stay that wonder was to see:
But, when I fear'd, he held me by the hand.
Through great deserts we wandered on our way—
Forward we passed on narrow bridge of trie,
O'er waters great, which hediously did roar."

Again, she supposes herself suspended over an infernal gulf:—

> " Ere I was ware, one gripp'd me at the last,
> And held me high above a flaming fire.
> The fire was great ; the heat did pierce me sore ;
> My faith grew weak ; my grip was very small ;
> I trembled fast ; my fear grew more and more."

A horrible picture of the same kind, dictated probably by the author's unhappy state of mind, is to be found in Brooke's *Fool of Quality*. The dreamer, a ruined female, is suspended over the gulf of perdition by a single hair, which is severed by a demon, who, in the form of her seducer, springs upwards from the flames.

The Russian funeral service, without any allegorical imagery, expresses the sentiment of the dirge in language alike simple and noble. " Hast thou pitied the afflicted, O man ? In death shalt thou be pitied. Hast thou consoled the orphan ? The orphan will deliver thee. Hast thou clothed the naked ? The naked will procure thee protection."—RICHARDSON'S *Anecdotes of Russia*.

But the most minute description of the *Brig o' Dread* occurs in the legend of *Sir Owain*, No. XL. in the MS. Collection of Romances, W. 4. 1. Advocates' Library, Edinburgh : though its position is not the same as in the dirge, which may excite a suspicion that the order of the stanzas in the latter has been transposed. Sir Owain, a Northumbrian knight, after many frightful adventures in St Patrick's purgatory, at last arrives at the bridge, which, in the legend, is placed betwixt purgatory and paradise:—

> " The fendes han the knight ynome,[1]
> To a stinkand water thai ben ycome,
>   He no seigh never er[2] non swiche;
> It stank fouler than ani hounde,
> And mani mile it was to the grounde,
>   And was as swart as piche.
>
> " And Owain seigh ther ouer ligge
> A swithe strong naru brigge:
>   The fendes seyd tho;[3]
> ' Lo! Sir Knight, sestow[4] this?
> This is the brigge of paradis,
>   Here over thou must go.
>
> " ' And we thee schal with stones prowe,
> And the winde thee schal over blow,
>   And wirche thee full wo;
> Thou no schalt for all this unduerd,
> But gif thou falle a midwerd,
>   To our fewes[5] mo.
>
> " ' And when thou art adown yfalle,
> Than schal com our felawes alle,
>   And with her[6] hokes thee hede;
> We schal thee teche a newe play:
> Thou hast served us mani a day,
>   And into helle thee lede.'—
>
> " Owain biheld the brigge smert,
> The water ther under blac and swert,

---

[1] *Ynome*—took.—[2] *Seigh never er*—saw never before.—[3] *Tho*—then.—
[4] *Sestow*—see'st thou.—[5] *Fewes*—probably contracted for fellowes.—
[6] *Her*—their.

And sore him gan to drede;
For of othing¹ he tok yeme,²
    Never mot, in some beme,
        Thicker than the fendes yede.³

" The brigge was as heigh as a tour,
And as scharpe as a rasour,
    And naru it was also;
And the water that ther ran under,
Brend o' lightning and of thonder,
    That thocht him michel wo.

" Ther nis no clerk may write with ynke,
No no man no may bethink,
    No no mainter deuine;
That is ymade forsooth ywis,
Under the brigge of paradis,
    Halvendel the pine..

" So the dominical ous telle,
Ther is the pure entrae of helle,
    Seine Poule berth witnesse;⁴
Whoso falleth of the brigge adown,
Of him nis no redempcioun,
    Noither more nor lesse.

" The fendes seyd to the knight tho,
' Ouer this brigge might thou nowght go,
    For noneskines nede;⁵
Flee peril, sorwe, and wo,
And to that stede⁶ ther thou com fro,
    Wel fair we schal thee lede.'—

" Owain anon began bithenche,
Fram hou mani of the fendes wrenche,

¹ *Othing*—one thing.—² *Yeme*—aim; notice.—³ *Yede*—went.—⁴ The reader will probably search St Paul in vain for the evidence here referred to.—⁵ No kind of necessity.—⁶ *Stede*—dwelling.

>   God him saved hadde ;
> He sett his fot upon the brigge,
> No feld he no scharpe egge,
>   No nothing him no dred.
>
> " When the fendes yseigh tho,
> That he was more than half ygo,
>   Loude they gun to crie ;
> ' Allas ! allas ! that he was born !
> This ich knight we have forlorn
>   Out of our baylie.' "—[1]

The author of the *Legend of Sir Owain*, though a zealous Catholic, has embraced, in the fullest extent, the Talmudic doctrine of an earthly paradise, distinct from the celestial abode of the just, and serving as a place of initiation, preparatory to perfect bliss, and to the beatific vision.—See the Rabbi Menasse ben Israel, in a treatise called *Nishmath Chajim*, i. e. The Breath of Life.[2]

---

[1] *Baylie*—jurisdiction.

[2] [The reader is requested to compare this " Lyke-wake Dirge," with the chant to the parting spirit in Guy Mannering.—ED.]

A LYKE-WAKE DIRGE.

This ae nighte, this ae nighte,
   Every night and alle;
Fire and sleete, and candle lighte,
   And Christe receive thye saule.

When thou from hence away are paste,
   Every night and alle;
To Whinny-muir thou comest at laste;
   And Christe receive thye saule.

If ever thou gavest hosen and shoon,
   Every night and alle;
Sit thee down and put them on;
   And Christe receive thye saule.

If hosen and shoon thou ne'er gavest nane,
   Every night and alle;
The whinnes shall pricke thee to the bare bone:
   And Christe receive thye saule.

From Whinny-muir when thou mayst passe,
   Every night and alle;

To Brigg o' Dread thou comest at laste ;
And Christe receive thye saule.

* * * * * *

(*A stanza wanting.*)

From Brigg o' Dread when thou mayst passe,
   Every night and alle ;
To purgatory fire thou comest at laste ;
   And Christe receive thye saule.

If ever thou gavest meat or drink,
   Every night and alle ;
The fire shall never make thee shrinke ;
   And Christe receive thye saule.

If meate or drinke thou never gavest nane,
   Every night and alle ;
The fire will burn thee to the bare bane ;
   And Christe receive thye saule.

This ae nighte, this ae nighte,
   Every night and alle ;
Fire and sleete, and candle lighte,
   And Christe receive thye saule.

THE DOWIE DENS O' YARROW, CONTINUED.

THE DOWIE DENS O' YARROW, CONTINUED.

THE DOWIE DENS O' YARROW, CONTINUED.

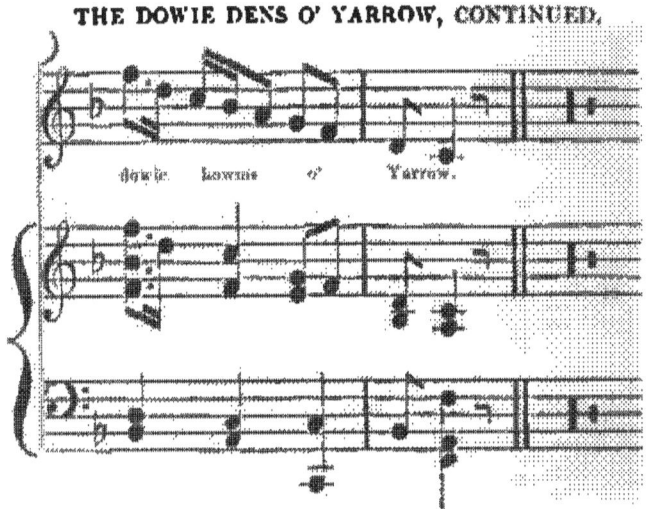

THE
DOWIE DENS OF YARROW.

NOW FIRST PUBLISHED.

This ballad, which is a very great favourite among the inhabitants of Ettrick Forest, is universally believed to be founded in fact. I found it easy to collect a variety of copies; but very difficult indeed to select from them such a collated edition, as might, in any degree, suit the taste of "these more light and giddy-paced times."

Tradition places the event, recorded in the song, very early; and it is probable that the ballad was composed soon afterwards, although the language has been gradually modernized, in the course of its transmission to us, through the inaccurate channel of oral tradition. The bard does not relate particulars, but barely the striking outlines of a fact, apparently so well known when he wrote, as to render minute detail as unnecessary, as it is always tedious and unpoetical.

The hero of the ballad was a knight of great bravery,

called Scott, who is said to have resided at Kirkhope, or Oakwood Castle, and is, in tradition, termed the Baron of Oakwood. The estate of Kirkhope belonged anciently to the Scotts of Harden: Oakwood is still their property, and has been so from time immemorial. The Editor was therefore led to suppose, that the hero of the ballad might have been identified with John Scott, sixth son of the Laird of Harden, murdered in Ettrick Forest by his kinsmen, the Scotts of Gilmanscleugh. (See notes to *Jamie Telfer, ante.*) This appeared the more probable, as the common people always affirm that this young man was treacherously slain, and that, in evidence thereof, his body remained uncorrupted for many years; so that even the roses on his shoes seemed as fresh as when he was first laid in the family vault at Hassendean. But from a passage in Nisbet's Heraldry, he now believes the ballad refers to a duel fought at Deucharswyre, of which Annan's Treat is a part, betwixt John Scott of Tushielaw and his brother-in-law, Walter Scott, third son of Robert of Thirlestane, in which the latter was slain.

In ploughing Annan's Treat, a huge monumental stone, with an inscription, was discovered; but being rather scratched than engraved, and the lines being run through each other, it is only possible to read one or two Latin words. It probably records the event of the combat. The person slain was the male ancestor of the present Lord Napier.

Tradition affirms, that the hero of the song (be he

who he may) was murdered by the brother, either of his wife or betrothed bride. The alleged cause of malice was the lady's father having proposed to endow her with half of his property, upon her marriage with a warrior of such renown. The name of the murderer is said to have been Annan, and the place of combat is still called Annan's Treat. It is a low muir, on the banks of the Yarrow, lying to the west of Yarrow Kirk. Two tall unhewn masses of stone are erected, about eighty yards distant from each other; and the least child, that can herd a cow, will tell the passenger, that there lie "the two lords, who were slain in single combat."

It will be, with many readers, the greatest recommendation of these verses, that they are supposed to have suggested to Mr Hamilton of Bangour, the modern ballad, beginning,

"Busk ye, busk ye, my bonny bonny bride."[1]

A fragment, apparently regarding the story of the

[1] [It may now be added, that Hamilton's ballad, and the scenery of the tragic tale, have inspired Mr Wordsworth to two of his most exquisite poems—"Yarrow Unvisited," and "Yarrow Visited;" and that he has more lately immortalized an excursion to the Yarrow, in which he was accompanied by Sir Walter Scott, only two days before Sir Walter left Scotland in September, 1831, in a most affecting piece, not yet published, entitled, "Yarrow Revisited."—ED.]

following ballad, but in a different measure, occurs in Mr Herd's MS., and runs thus:—

> "When I look east, my heart is sair,
> But when I look west, it's mair and mair;
> For then I see the braes o' Yarrow,
> And there, for aye, I lost my marrow."

THE DOWIE DENS OF YARROW.[1]

Late at e'en, drinking the wine,
  And ere they paid the lawing,
They set a combat them between,
  To fight it in the dawing.

" O stay at hame, my noble lord,
  O stay at hame, my marrow!
My cruel brother will you betray
  On the dowie houms of Yarrow."—

" O fare ye weel, my ladye gaye!
  O fare ye weel, my Sarah!
For I maun gae, though I ne'er return
  Frae the dowie banks o' Yarrow."

She kiss'd his cheek, she kaim'd his hair,
  As oft she had done before, O;

[1] [*Dowie*—means *melancholy*.
  " Meek loveliness is round thee spread,
    A softness still and holy—
  The grace of forest charms decayed,
    And pastoral melancholy."
            Yarrow Visited.]

She belted him with his noble brand,
    And he's away to Yarrow.

As he gaed up the Tennies bank,[1]
    I wot he gaed wi' sorrow,
Till, down in a den, he spied nine arm'd men,
    On the dowie houms of Yarrow.

" O come ye here to part your land,
    The bonnie Forest thorough?
Or come ye here to wield your brand,
    On the dowie houms of Yarrow?"—

" I come not here to part my land,
    And neither to beg nor borrow;
I come to wield my noble brand,
    On the bonnie banks of Yarrow.

" If I see all, ye're nine to ane;
    And that's an unequal marrow;
Yet will I fight, while lasts my brand,
    On the bonnie banks of Yarrow."

Four has he hurt, and five has slain,
    On the bloody braes of Yarrow,
Till that stubborn knight came him behind,
    And ran his body thorough.

---

[1] [*The Tennies* is the name of a farm of the Duke of Buccleuch's, a little below Yarrow Kirk.]

" Gae hame, gae hame, good-brother[1] John,
   And tell your sister Sarah,
To come and lift her leafu' lord;
   He's sleepin sound on Yarrow."—

" Yestreen I dream'd a dolefu' dream;
   I fear there will be sorrow!
I dream'd I pu'd the heather green,
   Wi' my true love, on Yarrow.

" O gentle wind, that bloweth south,
   From where my love repaireth,
Convey a kiss from his dear mouth,
   And tell me how he fareth!

" But in the glen strive armed men;
   They've wrought me dole and sorrow;
They've slain—the comeliest knight they've slain—
   He bleeding lies on Yarrow."

As she sped down yon high high hill,
   She gaed wi' dole and sorrow,
And in the den spied ten slain men,
   On the dowie banks of Yarrow.

She kissed his cheek, she kaim'd his hair,
   She searched his wounds all thorough,

---

[1] *Good-brother*—Beau-frere; brother-in-law.

She kiss'd them, till her lips grew red,
    On the dowie houms of Yarrow.

" Now haud your tongue, my daughter dear!
    For a' this breeds but sorrow;
I'll wed ye to a better lord,
    Than him ye lost on Yarrow."—

" O haud your tongue, my father dear!
    Ye mind me but of sorrow;
A fairer rosé did never bloom
    Than now lies cropp'd on Yarrow."

THE GAY GOSS-HAWK.

NEVER BEFORE PUBLISHED.

This Ballad is published, partly from one, under this title, in Mrs Brown's Collection, and partly from a MS. of some antiquity, penes Edit.—The stanzas appearing to possess most merit, have been selected from each copy.

    " O WALY, waly, my gay goss-hawk,
       Gin your feathering be sheen!"—
    " And waly, waly, my master dear,
       Gin ye look pale and lean!

    " O have ye tint, at tournament,
       Your sword, or yet your spear?
    Or mourn ye for the southern lass,
       Whom ye may not win near?"—

    " I have not tint, at tournament,
       My sword nor yet my spear;
    But sair I mourn for my true love,
       Wi' mony a bitter tear.

"But weel's me on ye, my gay goss-hawk,
    Ye can baith speak and flee;
Ye sall carry a letter to my love,
    Bring an answer back to me."—

"But how sall I your true love find,
    Or how suld I her know?
I bear a tongue ne'er wi' her spake,
    An eye that ne'er her saw."—

"O weel sall ye my true love ken,
    Sae sune as ye her see;
For, of a' the flowers of fair England,
    The fairest flower is she.

"The red, that's on my true love's cheek,
    Is like blood-drops on the snaw;[1]
The white, that is on her breast bare,
    Like the down o' the white sea-maw.

---

[1] This simile resembles a passage in a MS. translation of an Irish Fairy tale, called *The Adventures of Faravla, Princess of Scotland, and Carral O'Daly, Son of Donogho More O'Daly, Chief Bard of Ireland.* "Faravla, as she entered her bower, cast her looks upon the earth, which was tinged with the blood of a bird which a raven had newly killed: 'Like that snow,' said Faravla, 'was the complexion of my beloved, his cheeks like the sanguine traces thereon; whilst the raven recalls to my memory the colour of his beautiful locks.'" There is also some resemblance in the conduct of the story, betwixt the ballad and the tale just quoted. The Princess Faravla, being desperately in love with Carral

" And even at my love's bour-door
  There grows a flowering birk ;
And ye maun sit and sing thereon
  As she gangs to the kirk.

" And four-and-twenty fair ladyes
  Will to the mass repair ;
But weel may ye my ladye ken,
  The fairest ladye there."

Lord William has written a love-letter,
  Put it under his pinion gray ;
And he is awa to Southern land
  As fast as wings can gae.

And even at the ladye's bour
  There grew a flowering birk ;
And he sat down and sung thereon
  As she gaed to the kirk.

And weel he kent that ladye fair
  Amang her maidens free ;

O'Daly, despatches in search of him a faithful confidante, who, by her magical art, transforms herself into a hawk, and, perching upon the windows of the bard, conveys to him information of the distress of the Princess of Scotland.

In the ancient romance of *Sir Tristrem*, the simile of the "blood-drops upon snow" likewise occurs :—

" A bride bright that ches
  As blod opon snoweing."

For the flower, that springs in May morning,
    Was not sae sweet as she.

He lighted at the ladye's yate,
    And sat him on a pin;
And sang fu' sweet the notes o' love,
    Till a' was cosh¹ within.

And first he sang a low low note,
    And syne he sang a clear;
And aye the o'erword o' the sang
    Was—" Your love can no win here."—

" Feast on, feast on, my maidens a',
    The wine flows you amang,
While I gang to my shot-window,²
    And hear yon bonny bird's sang.

" Sing on, sing on, my bonny bird,
    The sang ye sung yestreen;
For weel I ken, by your sweet singing,
    Ye are frae my true love sen."

O first he sang a merry sang,
    And syne he sang a grave;
And syne he pick'd his feathers gray,
    To her the letter gave.

---

¹ *Cosh*—quiet.—² *Shot-window*—A bow-window.

" Have there a letter from Lord William ;
　　He says he's sent ye three ;
He canna wait your love langer,
　　But for your sake he'll die."—

" Gae bid him bake his bridal bread,
　　And brew his bridal ale ;
And I shall meet him at Mary's kirk,
　　Lang, lang ere it be stale."

The lady's gane to her chamber,
　　And a moanfu' woman was she ;
As gin she had ta'en a sudden brash,[1]
　　And were about to die.

" A boon, a boon, my father deir,
　　A boon I beg of thee !"—
" Ask not that paughty Scottish lord,
　　For him you ne'er shall see.

" But, for your honest asking else,
　　Weel granted it shall be."—
" Then, gin I die in Southern land,
　　In Scotland gar bury me.

" And the first kirk that ye come to,
　　Ye's gar the mass be sung ;

---

[1] *Brash—sickness.*

And the next kirk that ye come to,
　　Ye's gar the bells be rung.

" And when ye come to St Mary's kirk,
　　Ye's tarry there till night."
And so her father pledg'd his word,
　　And so his promise plight.

She has ta'en her to her bigly bour
　　As fast as she could fare;
And she has drank a sleepy draught,
　　That she had mix'd wi' care.

And pale, pale grew her rosy cheek,
　　That was sae bright of blee,[1]
And she seem'd to be as surely dead
　　As any one could be.

Then spake her cruel step-minnie,
　　" Tak ye the burning lead,
And drap a drap on her bosome,
　　To try if she be dead."

They took a drap o' boiling lead,
　　They drapp'd it on her breast;
" Alas! alas!" her father cried,
　　" She's dead without the priest."

[1] *Blee*—bloom.

She neither chatter'd with her teeth,
    Nor shiver'd with her chin;
"Alas! alas!" her father cried,
    "There is nae breath within."

Then up arose her seven brethren,
    And hew'd to her a bier;
They hew'd it frae the solid aik,
    Laid it o'er wi' silver clear.

"Then up and gat her seven sisters,
    And sewed to her a kell;[1]
And every steek that they put in
    Sewed to a siller bell.

The first Scots kirk that they cam to,
    They garr'd the bells be rung;
The next Scots kirk that they cam to,
    They garr'd the mass be sung.

But when they cam to St Mary's kirk,
    There stude spearmen all on a raw;
And up and started Lord William,
    The chieftane amang them a'.

"Set down, set down the bier," he said
    "Let me look her upon:"

[1] *Kell*—shroud.

But as soon as Lord William touch'd her hand,
  Her colour began to come.

She brightened like the lily flower,
  Till her pale colour was gone;
With rosy cheek, and ruby lip,
  She smiled her love upon.

" A morsel of your bread, my lord,
  And one glass of your wine;
For I hae fasted these three lang days,
  All for your sake and mine.—

" Gae hame, gae hame, my seven bauld brothers
  Gae hame and blaw your horn!
I trow ye wad hae gi'en me the skaith,
  But I've gi'en you the scorn.

" Commend me to my grey father,
  That wished my saul gude rest;
But wae be to my cruel step-dame,
  Garr'd burn me on the breast."—

" Ah! woe to you, you light woman!
  An ill death may ye die!
For we left father and sisters at hame
  Breaking their hearts for thee."[1]

---

[1] [The reader will find another version of this ballad in Motherwell's Collection, 1827, p. 353.—ED.]

BROWN ADAM.

There is a copy of this Ballad in Mrs BROWN's Collection. The Editor has seen one, printed on a single sheet. The epithet, "Smith," implies, probably, the sirname, not the profession, of the hero, who seems to have been an outlaw. There is, however, in Mrs BROWN's copy, a verse of little merit, here omitted, alluding to the implements of that occupation.

O WHA wad wish the wind to blaw,
   Or the green leaves fa' therewith?
Or wha wad wish a lealer love
   Than Brown Adam the Smith?

But they hae banished him, Brown Adam,
   Frae father and frae mother;
And they hae banish'd him, Brown Adam,
   Frae sister and frae brother.

And they hae banish'd him, Brown Adam,
   The flower o' a' his kin;
And he's bigged a bour in gude green-wood
   Atween his ladye and him.

It fell upon a summer's day,
   Brown Adam he thought lang;
And, for to hunt some venison,
   To green-wood he wald gang.

He has ta'en his bow his arm o'er,
   His bolts and arrows lang;
And he is to the gude green-wood
   As fast as he could gang.

O he's shot up, and he's shot down,
   The bird upon the brier;
And he sent it hame to his ladye,
   Bade her be of gude cheir.

O he's shot up, and he's shot down,
   The bird upon the thorn;
And sent it hame to his ladye,
   Said he'd be hame the morn.

When he cam to his lady's bour door
   He stude a little forbye,
And there he heard a fou fause knight
   Tempting his gay ladye.

For he's ta'en out a gay goud ring,
   Had cost him many a poun',
"O grant me love for love, ladye,
   And this sall be thy own."—

"I lo'e Brown Adam weel," she said;
 "I trew sae does he me;
I wadna gie Brown Adam's love
 For nae fause knight I see."—

Out has he ta'en a purse o' gowd,
 Was a' fou to the string,
"O grant me love for love, ladye,
 And a' this sall be thine."—

"I lo'e Brown Adam weel," she says;
 "I wot sae does he me:
I wadna be your light leman,
 For mair than ye could gie."—

Then out he drew his lang bright brand,
 And flash'd it in her een;
"Now grant me love for love, ladye,
 Or thro' ye this sall gang!"—
Then, sighing, says that ladye fair,
 "Brown Adam tarries lang!"—

Then in and starts him Brown Adam,
 Says—"I'm just at your hand."—
He's gar'd him leave his bonny bow,
 He's gar'd him leave his brand,
He's gar'd him leave a dearer pledge—
 Four fingers o' his right hand.

JELLON GRAME.

NEVER BEFORE PUBLISHED.

This ballad is published from tradition, with some conjectural emendations. It is corrected by a copy in Mrs Brown's MS., from which it differs in the concluding stanzas. Some verses are apparently modernized.

Jellon seems to be the same name with *Jyllian* or *Julian*. "Jyl of Brentford's Testament" is mentioned in Warton's *History of Poetry*, vol. ii. p. 40. The name repeatedly occurs in old ballads, sometimes as that of a man, at other times as that of a woman. Of the former is an instance in the ballad of "*The Knight and the Shepherd's Daughter.*"—*Reliques of Ancient Poetry*, vol. iii. p. 72:

> " Some do call me Jack, sweetheart,
> And some do call me *Jille*."

Witton Gilbert, a village four miles west of Durham, is, throughout the bishopric, pronounced Witton Jilbert. We have also the common name of Giles, always in Scotland pronounced Jill. For Gille, or

Juliana, as a female name, we have *Fair Gillian* of Croyden, and a thousand authorities. Such being the case, the Editor must enter his protest against the conversion of *Gil* Morrice into *Child* Maurice, an epithet of chivalry. All the circumstances in that ballad argue, that the unfortunate hero was an obscure and very young man, who had never received the honour of knighthood. At any rate, there can be no reason, even were internal evidence totally wanting, for altering a well-known proper name, which, till of late years, has been the uniform title of the ballad.

JELLON GRAME.

O JELLON GRAME sat in Silverwood,[1]
    He sharp'd his broadsword lang;
And he has call'd his little foot-page
    An errand for to gang.

"Win up, my bonny boy," he says,
    "As quickly as ye may;
For ye maun gang for Lillie Flower
    Before the break of day."—

The boy has buckled his belt about,
    And through the green-wood ran;
And he came to the ladye's bower
    Before the day did dawn.

"O sleep ye, wake ye, Lillie Flower?
    The red sun's on the rain:

---

[1] Silverwood, mentioned in this ballad, occurs in a medley MS. song, which seems to have been copied from the first edition of the Aberdeen cantus, *penes* John G. Dalyell, Esq. advocate. One line only is cited, apparently the beginning of some song:—
    "Silverwood, gin ye were mine."

Ye're bidden come to Silverwood,
    But I doubt ye'll never win hame."—

She hadna ridden a mile, a mile,
    A mile but barely three,
Ere she came to a new-made grave,
    Beneath a green aik tree.

O then up started Jellon Grame,
    Out of a bush thereby;
"Light down, light down, now, Lillie Flower,
    For it's here that ye maun lye."—

She lighted aff her milk-white steed,
    And kneel'd upon her knee;
"O mercy, mercy, Jellon Grame,
    For I'm no prepared to die!

"Your bairn, that stirs between my sides,
    Maun shortly see the light:
But to see it weltering in my blood,
    Would be a piteous sight."—

"O should I spare your life," he says,
    "Until that bairn were born,
Full weel I ken your auld father
    Would hang me on the morn."—

"O spare my life, now, Jellon Grame!
    My father ye needna dread:

I'll keep my babe in gude green-wood,
   Or wi' it I'll beg my bread."—

He took no pity on Lillie Flower,
   Though she for life did pray;
But pierced her through the fair body
   As at his feet she lay.

He felt nae pity for Lillie Flower,
   Where she was lying dead;
But he felt some for the bonny bairn,
   That lay weltering in her bluid.

Up has he ta'en that bonny boy,
   Given him to nurses nine;
Three to sleep, and three to wake,
   And three to go between.

And he bred up that bonny boy,
   Call'd him his sister's son:
And he thought no eye could ever see
   The deed that he had done.

O so it fell upon a day,
   When hunting they might be,
They rested them in Silverwood,
   Beneath that green aik tree.

And many were the green-wood flowers
   Upon the grave that grew,

And marvell'd much that bonny boy
   To see their lovely hue.

"What's paler than the prymrose wan?
   What's redder than the rose?
What's fairer than the lilye flower
   On this wee know[1] that grows?"—

O out and answer'd Jellon Grame,
   And he spak hastilie—
"Your mother was a fairer flower,
   And lies beneath this tree.

"More pale she was, when she sought my grace,
   Than prymrose pale and wan;
And redder than rose her ruddy heart's blood,
   That down my broadsword ran."—

Wi' that the boy has bent his bow,
   It was baith stout and lang;
And thro' and thro' him, Jellon Grame,
   He gar'd an arrow gang.

Says,—"Lie ye there, now, Jellon Grame!
   My malisoun gang you wi'!
The place that my mother lies buried in
   Is far too good for thee."—

    [1] *Wee know*—Little hillock.

WILLIE'S LADYE.

ANCIENT COPY.

NEVER BEFORE PUBLISHED.

Mr Lewis, in his *Tales of Wonder*, has presented the public with a copy of this ballad, with additions and alterations. The Editor has also seen a copy, containing some modern stanzas, intended by Mr Jamieson, of Macclesfield, for publication in his Collection of Scottish Poetry.[1] Yet, under these disadvantages, the Editor cannot relinquish his purpose of publishing the old ballad, in its native simplicity, as taken from Mrs Brown of Falkland's MS.

Those who wish to know how an incantation, or charm, of the distressing nature here described, was performed in classic days, may consult the story of Galanthis's Metamorphosis, in Ovid, or the following passage in Apuleius: "*Eadem (Saga scilicet quæ-*

---

[1] Edit. 1802. Mr Jamieson's interesting Collection has since been published. 1810.

dam,) amatoris uxorem, quod in eam dicacule probrum dixerat, jam in sarcinam prægnationis, obsepto utero, et repigrato fœtu, perpetua prægnatione damnavit. Et ut cuncti numerant, octo annorum onere, misella illa, velut elephantum paritura, distenditur."—Apul. *Metam.* lib. 1.

There is also a curious tale about a Count of Westeravia, whom a deserted concubine bewitched upon his marriage, so as to preclude all hopes of his becoming a father. The spell continued to operate for three years, till one day, the Count happening to meet with his former mistress, she maliciously asked him about the increase of his family. The Count, conceiving some suspicion from her manner, craftily answered, that God had blessed him with three fine children; on which she exclaimed, like Willie's mother in the ballad, " May Heaven confound the old hag, by whose counsel I threw an enchanted pitcher into the draw-well of your palace!" The spell being found, and destroyed, the Count became the father of a numerous family.—*Hierarchie of the Blessed Angels,* p. 474.

WILLIE'S LADYE.

Willie's ta'en him o'er the faem,[1]
He's wooed a wife, and brought her hame;
He's wooed her for her yellow hair,
But his mother wrought her meikle care;

And meikle dolour gar'd her dree,
For lighter she can never be;
But in her bower she sits wi' pain,
And Willie mourns o'er her in vain.

And to his mother he has gane,
That vile rank witch, o' vilest kind!
He says—" My ladie has a cup,
Wi' gowd and silver set about;
This gudely gift sall be your ain,
And let her be lighter o' her young bairn."—

" Of her young bairn she's never be lighter,
Nor in her bour to shine the brighter:

[1] *Faem*—The sea foam.

But she sall die, and turn to clay,
And you sall wed another may."—

" Another may I'll never wed,
Another may I'll never bring hame."—
But, sighing, said that weary wight—
" I wish my life were at an end!

" Yet gae ye to your mother again,
That vile rank witch, o' vilest kind!
And say, your ladye has a steed,
The like o' him's no in the land o' Leed.[1]

" For he is silver shod before,
And he is gowden shod behind;
At every tuft of that horse mane,
There's a golden chess,[2] and a bell to ring.
This gudely gift sall be her ain,
And let me be lighter o' my young bairn."—

" Of her young bairn she's ne'er be lighter,
Nor in her bour to shine the brighter;
But she sall die, and turn to clay,
And ye sall wed another may."—

" Another may I'll never wed,
Another may I'll never bring hame."—

[1] *Land o' Leed*—Perhaps Lydia.
[2] *Chess*—Should probably be *jess*, the name of a hawk's bell.

But, sighing, said that weary wight—
"I wish my life were at an end!"—

"Yet gae ye to your mother again,
That vile rank witch, o' rankest kind!
And say your ladye has a girdle,
It's a' red gowd to the middle;

"And aye, at ilka siller hem
Hang fifty siller bells and ten;
This gudely gift sall be her ain,
And let me be lighter o' my young bairn."—

"Of her young bairn she's ne'er be lighter,
Nor in your bour to shine the brighter;
For she sall die, and turn to clay,
And thou sall wed another may."—

"Another may I'll never wed,
Another may I'll never bring hame."—
But, sighing, said that weary wight—
"I wish my days were at an end!"—

Then out and spak the Billy Blind,[1]
(He spak aye in good time:)

---

[1] *Billy Blind.*—A familiar genius, or propitious spirit, somewhat similar to the *Brownie.* He is mentioned repeatedly in Mrs Brown's Ballads, but I have not met with him anywhere else, although he is alluded to in the rustic game of Bogle (i. e. *goblin*) *Billy Blind.*

" Yet gae ye to the market-place,
And there do buy a loaf of wace ;[1]
Do shape it bairn and bairnly like,
And in it twa glassen een you'll put ;

" And bid her your boy's christening to,
Then notice weel what she shall do ;
And do you stand a little away,
To notice weel what she may say."
  *   *   *   *

[*A stanza seems to be wanting. Willie is supposed to follow the advice of the spirit.—His mother speaks.*]

" O wha has loosed the nine witch knots,
That were amang that ladye's locks ?
And wha's ta'en out the kaims o' care,
That were amang that ladye's hair ?

" And wha has ta'en down that bush o' woodbine,
That hung between her bour and mine ?
And wha has kill'd the master kid,
That ran beneath that ladye's bed ?
And wha has loosed her left foot shee,
And let that ladye lighter be ?"

The word is, indeed, used in Sir David Lindsay's plays, but apparently in a different sense—

" Priests sall leid you like ane *Billy Blinde*."

PINKERTON's *Scottish Poems*, 1792, vol. ii. p. 232.

[1] *Wace*—WAX.

Syne, Willy's loosed the nine witch knots,
That were amang that ladye's locks;
And Willie's ta'en out the kaims o' care,
That were into that ladye's hair;
And he's ta'en down the bush o' woodbine,
Hung atween her bour and the witch carline;

And he has kill'd the master kid,
That ran beneath that ladye's bed;
And he has loosed her left foot shee,
And latten that ladye lighter be;
And now he has gotten a bonny son,
And meikle grace be him upon.

CLERK SAUNDERS.

NEVER BEFORE PUBLISHED.

This romantic ballad is taken from Mr Herd's MSS., with several corrections from a shorter and more imperfect copy, in the same volume, and one or two conjectural emendations in the arrangement of the stanzas. The resemblance of the conclusion to the ballad, beginning, "There came a ghost to Margaret's door," will strike every reader. The tale is uncommonly wild and beautiful, and apparently very ancient. The custom of the passing bell is still kept up in many villages in Scotland. The sexton goes through the town, ringing a small bell, and announcing the death of the departed, and the time of the funeral.

The three concluding verses have been recovered since the first edition of this work: and I am informed by the reciter, that it was usual to separate from the rest, that part of the ballad which follows the death of the lovers, as belonging to another story. For this, however, there seems no necessity, as other authorities give the whole as a complete tale.[1]

[1] [Mr Kinloch has again separated the parts in his edition. See his Ballads, 1827, p. 240.—ED.]

CLERK SAUNDERS.[1]

Clerk Saunders and may Margaret
  Walked ower yon garden green;
And sad and heavy was the love
  That fell thir twa between.

[1] ["Two different copies of this pathetic and deeply-interesting ballad have been published: the one by the author of the *Border Minstrelsy*, and the other by Mr Jamieson, which, though of inferior beauty, is not the less valuable, as illustrating the transmutations to which traditionary song is inevitably subjected. To the copy we have adopted, we were almost inclined to prefix the following verses, which begin the copy preserved by Mr Jamieson:—

" Clerk Saunders was an earl's son,
  He lived upon sea sand;
May Margaret was a king's daughter,
  She liv'd in upper land.

" Clerk Saunders was an earl's son,
  Weel learned at the scheel;
May Margaret was a king's daughter,
  They baith lo'ed ither weel."—

because they supply information as to the rank in society respectively held by these ill-fated lovers—and, by hinting at the scholastic acquirements of Clerk Saunders, they prepare us for the casuistry by which he seeks to reconcile May Margaret's conscience to a most jesuitical oath."—Motherwell's *Minstrelsy*, p. 147-8.

A third copy has since been published by Buchan, under the title of "Clerk Sandy;" but his various readings are mere housemaid's corruptions. A fourth and more valuable set has also been given by Mr Kinloch.—Ed.]

" A bed, a bed," Clerk Saunders said,
  " A bed for you and me!"—
" Fye na, fye na," said may Margaret,
  " Till anes we married be;

" For in may come my seven bauld brothers,
  Wi' torches burning bright;
They'll say—' We hae but ae sister,
  And behold she's wi' a knight!' "—

" Then take the sword from my scabbard,
  And slowly lift the pin;
And you may swear, and safe your aith,
  Ye never let Clerk Saunders in.

" And take a napkin in your hand,
  And tie up baith your bonny een;
And you may swear, and safe your aith,
  Ye saw me na since late yestreen."—[1]

It was about the midnight hour,
  When they asleep were laid,

[1] [In the north-country version of this ballad, published by Mr Kinloch, we have an additional stanza here.—

——" Ye'll tak me in your arms twa,
Ye'll carry me into your bed,
And ye may swear, and save your aith,
That in your bour floor I ne'er gae'd."
                            KINLOCH, p. 235.—ED.]

When in and came her seven brothers,
    Wi' torches burning red.

When in and came her seven brothers,
    Wi' torches burning bright;
They said, "We hae but ae sister,
    And behold her lying with a knight!"

Then out and spake the first o' them,
    "I bear the sword shall gar him die!"
And out and spake the second o' them,
    "His father has nae mair than he!"

And out and spake the third o' them,
    "I wot that they are lovers dear!"
And out and spake the fourth o' them,
    "They hae been in love this mony a year!"

Then out and spake the fifth o' them,
    "It were great sin true love to twain!"
And out and spake the sixth of them,
    "It were shame to slay a sleeping man!"

Then up and gat the seventh o' them,
    And never a word spake he;
But he has striped[1] his bright brown brand
    Out through Clerk Saunders' fair bodye.

---

[1] *Striped*—Thrust.

Clerk Saunders he started, and Margaret she turn'd[1]
   Into his arms as asleep she lay;
And sad and silent was the night
   That was atween thir twae.

And they lay still and sleeped sound,
   Until the day began to daw;
And kindly to him she did say,
   " It is time, true love, you were awa."

But he lay still, and sleeped sound,
   Albeit the sun began to sheen;
She looked atween her and the wa',
   And dull and drowsie were his een.

Then in and came her father dear,
   Said—" Let a' your mourning be:
I'll carry the dead corpse to the clay,
   And I'll come back and comfort thee."—

" Comfort weel your seven sons,
   For comforted will I never be:

---

[1] [" Nothing could have been better imagined," says Mr Jamieson, " than the circumstance, in Mr Scott's copy, of killing Clerk Saunders while his mistress was asleep; nor can any thing be more natural or pathetic than the three stanzas that follow, beginning with,
   ' Clerk Saunders he started, and Margaret she turned,' &c.
They might have charmed a whole volume of bad poetry against the ravages of time. In Mr Scott's work, they shine but like pearls among diamonds."—*Jamieson's Ballads*, vol. i. p. 81.]

I ween 'twas neither knave nor loon
　　Was in the bower last night wi' me."—

The clinking bell gaed through the town,
　　To carry the dead corse to the clay;
And Clerk Saunders stood at may Margaret's window,
　　I wot, an hour before the day.

" Are ye sleeping, Margaret?" he says,
　　" Or are ye waking presentlie?
Give me my faith and troth again,
　　I wot, true love, I gied to thee."—

" Your faith and troth ye sall never get,
　　Nor our true love sall never twin,
Until ye come within my bower,
　　And kiss me cheik and chin."—

" My mouth it is full cold, Margaret,
　　It has the smell, now, of the ground;
And if I kiss thy comely mouth,
　　Thy days of life will not be lang.

" O, cocks are crowing a merry midnight,
　　I wot the wild fowls are boding day;
Give me my faith and troth again,
　　And let me fare me on my way."—

" Thy faith and troth thou sall na get,
　　And our true love shall never twin,

Until ye tell what comes of women,
  I wot, who die in strong traivelling?"[1]

"Their beds are made in the heavens high,
  Down at the foot of our good Lord's knee,
Weel set about wi' gillyflowers;[2]
  I wot sweet company for to see.

"O, cocks are crowing a merry midnight,
  I wot the wild fowl are boding day;

---

[1] *Traivelling*—Child-birth.

[2] From whatever source the popular ideas of heaven be derived, the mention of gillyflowers is not uncommon. Thus, in the Dead Men's Song—

  "The fields about this city faire
    Were all with roses set;
  Gillyflowers, and carnations faire,
    Which canker could not fret."
        Ritson's *Ancient Songs*, p. 290.

The description, given in the legend of *Sir Owain*, of the terrestrial paradise, at which the blessed arrive after passing through purgatory, omits gillyflowers, though it mentions many others. As the passage is curious, and the legend has never been published, many persons may not be displeased to see it extracted—

  "Fair were her erbers with flowres,
  Rose and lili divers colours,
    Primros and parvink:
  Mint, feverfoy, and eglanterre,
  Colombin, and mother wer
    Than ani man mai bithenke.
  It berth erbes of other maner,
  Than ani in erth groweth here,
    Tho that is lest of pris;
  Evermore that grene springeth,
  For winter no somer it no clingeth,
  And sweeter than licorice."

The psalms of heaven will soon be sung,
  And I, ere now, will be miss'd away."—

Then she has ta'en a crystal wand,
  And she has stroken her troth thereon;
She has given it him out at the shot-window,
  Wi' mony a sad sigh, and heavy groan.

" I thank ye, Marg'ret; I thank ye, Marg'ret;
  And aye I thank ye heartilie;
Gin ever the dead come for the quick,
  Be sure, Marg'ret, I'll come for thee."—

It's hosen and shoon, and gown alone,
  She climb'd the wall, and follow'd him,
Until she came to the green forest,
  And there she lost the sight o' him.

" Is there ony room at your head, Saunders?
  Is there ony room at your feet?
Or ony room at your side, Saunders,
  Where fain, fain, I wad sleep?"—

" There's nae room at my head, Marg'ret,
  There's nae room at my feet;
My bed it is full lowly now:
  Amang the hungry worms I sleep.

" Cauld mould is my covering now,
  But and my winding-sheet;

The dew it falls nae sooner down,
    Than my resting place is weet.

" But plait a wand o' bonny birk,[1]
    And lay it on my breast;
And shed a tear upon my grave,
    And wish my saul gude rest.

" And fair Marg'ret, and rare Marg'ret,
    And Marg'ret o' veritie,
Gin e'er ye love another man,
    Ne'er love him as ye did me."—

Then up and crew the milk-white cock,
    And up and crew the grey;
Her lover vanish'd in the air,
    And she gaed weeping away.

---

[1] The custom of binding the new-laid sod of the churchyard with osiers, or other saplings, prevailed both in England and Scotland, and served to protect the turf from injury by cattle, or otherwise. It is alluded to by Gay, in the *What d'ye call it*—

    " Stay, let me pledge, 'tis my last earthly liquor,
    When I am dead you'll bind my grave with *wicker*."

In the *Shepherd's Week*, the same custom is alluded to, and the cause explained:—

    " With *wicker rods* we fenced her tomb around,
    To ward, from man and beast, the hallow'd ground,
    Lest her new grave the parson's cattle raze,
    For both his horse and cow the churchyard graze."
                                      Fifth Pastoral.

EARL RICHARD.

NEVER BEFORE PUBLISHED.

There are two Ballads in Mr HERD's *MSS. upon the following story, in one of which the unfortunate Knight is termed* YOUNG HUNTIN.[1] *A fragment, containing from the sixth to the tenth verse, has been repeatedly published. The best verses are selected from both copies, and some trivial alterations have been adopted from tradition.*

" O LADY, rock never your young son young,
   One hour langer for me ;
For I have a sweetheart in Garlioch Wells
   I love far better than thee.

" The very sole o' that lady's foot
   Than thy face is far mair white."—
" But, nevertheless, now, Erl Richard,
   Ye will bide in my bower a' night ?"—

[1] [Mr Buchan has published (1828) a copy of " Young Huntin," as preserved in Aberdeenshire. See vol. i. p. 118.—ED.]

She birled[1] him with the ale and wine,
    As they sat down to sup:
A living man he laid him down,
    But I wot he ne'er rose up.

Then up and spake the popinjay,
    That flew aboun her head;
"Lady! keep weel your green cleiding
    Frae gude Erl Richard's bleid."—

"O better I'll keep my green cleiding
    Frae gude Erl Richard's bleid,
Than thou canst keep thy clattering toung,
    That trattles in thy head."

She has call'd upon her bower maidens,
    She has call'd them ane by ane;
"There lies a dead man in my bour:
    I wish that he were gane!"

They hae booted him, and spurred him,
    As he was wont to ride;—
A hunting-horn tied round his waist,
    A sharpe sword by his side;
And they hae had him to the wan water,
    For a' men call it Clyde.[2]

[1] *Birled*—Plied.—[2] [*Clyde*, in Celtic, means *white*.—ED.]

Then up and spoke the popinjay
  That sat upon the tree—
" What hae ye done wi' Erl Richard?
  Ye were his gay ladye."—

" Come down, come down, my bonny bird,
  And sit upon my hand;
And thou sall hae a cage o' gowd,
  Where thou hast but the wand."—

" Awa! awa! ye ill woman!
  Nae cage o' gowd for me;
As ye hae done to Erl Richard,
  Sae wad ye do to me."

She hadna cross'd a rigg o' land,
  A rigg but barely ane,
When she met wi' his auld father,
  Came riding all alane.

" Where hae ye been, now, ladye fair,
  Where hae ye been sae late?
We hae been seeking Erl Richard,
  But him we canna get."—

" Erl Richard kens a' the fords in Clyde,
  He'll ride them ane by ane.
And though the night was ne'er sae mirk,
  Erl Richard will be hame."

O it fell anes, upon a day,
    The King was boun to ride;
And he has mist him, Erl Richard,
    Should hae ridden on his right side.

The ladye turn'd her round about,
    Wi' mickle mournfu' din—
" It fears me sair o' Clyde water,
    That he is drown'd therein."—

" Gar douk, gar douk,"[1] the King he cried,
    " Gar douk for gold and fee;
O wha will douk for Erl Richard's sake,
    Or wha will douk for me?"

They douked in at ae weil-heid,[2]
    And out aye at the other;
" We can douk nae mair for Erl Richard,
    Although he were our brother."

It fell that, in that ladye's castle,
    The King was boun to bed;
And up and spake the popinjay,
    That flew abune his head.

" Leave aff your douking on the day,
    And douk upon the night;

---

[1] *Douk*—Dive.—[2] *Weil-heid*—Eddy.

And where that sackless[1] knight lies slain,
    The candles will burn bright."—

"O there's a bird within this bower,
    That sings baith sad and sweet;
O there's a bird within your bower,
    Keeps me frae my night's sleep."

They left the douking on the day,
    And douk'd upon the night;
And where that sackless knight lay slain,
    The candles burned bright.[2]

The deepest pot in a' the linn,[3]
    They fand Erl Richard in;

---

[1] *Sackless*—Guiltless.

[2] These are unquestionably the corpse-lights, called in Wales *Canhwyllan Cyrph*, which are sometimes seen to illuminate the spot where a dead body is concealed. The Editor is informed, that, some years ago, the corpse of a man, drowned in the Ettrick, below Selkirk, was discovered by means of these candles. Such lights are common in churchyards, and are probably of a phosphoric nature. But rustic superstition derives them from supernatural agency, and supposes, that, as soon as life has departed, a pale flame appears at the window of the house, in which the person had died, and glides towards the churchyard, tracing through every winding the route of the future funeral, and pausing where the bier is to rest. This and other opinions, relating to the "tomb-fires' livid gleam," seem to be of Runic extraction.

[3] The deep holes, scooped in the rock by the eddies of a river, are called *pots*; the motion of the water having there some resemblance to a boiling caldron. *Linn*, means the pool beneath a cataract.

THE SCOTTISH BORDER.

A green turf tyed across his breast,
  To keep that gude lord down.

Then up and spake the King himsell,
  When he saw the deadly wound—
" O wha has slain my right-hand man,
  That held my hawk and hound ?"—

Then up and spake the popinjay,
  Says—" What needs a' this din ?
It was his light leman took his life,
  And hided him in the linn."

Sae swore her by the grass sae grene,
  Sae did she by the corn,
She hadna seen him, Erl Richard,
  Since Moninday at morn.

" Put na the wite on me," she said ;
  " It was my may Catherine."
Then they hae cut baith fern and thorn,
  To burn that maiden in.

It wadna take upon her cheik,
  Nor yet upon her chin ;
Nor yet upon her yellow hair,
  To cleanse the deadly sin.

The maiden touch'd the clay-cauld corpse,
    A drap it never bled;
The ladye laid her hand on him,
    And soon the ground was red.

Out they hae ta'en her, may Catherine,
    And put her mistress in;
The flame tuik fast upon her cheik,
    Tuik fast upon her chin;
Tuik fast upon her faire body—
    She burn'd like hollin-green.[1]

---

[1] *Hollin-green*—Green holly. The lines immediately preceding, "The maiden touched," &c. and which are restored from tradition, refer to a superstition formerly received in most parts of Europe, and even resorted to by judicial authority, for the discovery of murder. In Germany, this experiment was called *bahr-recht*, or the law of the bier; because, the murdered body being stretched upon a bier, the suspected person was obliged to put one hand upon the wound, and the other upon the mouth of the deceased, and, in that posture, call upon heaven to attest his innocence. If, during this ceremony, the blood gushed from the mouth, nose, or wound, a circumstance not unlikely to happen in the course of shifting or stirring the body, it was held sufficient evidence of the guilt of the party.

The same singular kind of evidence, although reprobated by Malthaeus and Carpzovius, was admitted in the Scottish criminal courts, at the short distance of one century. My readers may be amused by the following instances:—

"The Laird of Auchindrane (Muir of Auchindrane in Ayrshire) was accused of a horrid and private murder, where there were no witnesses, and which the Lord had witnessed from heaven, singularly by his own hand, and proved the deed against him. The corpse of the man being buried in Girvan churchyard, as a man cast away at sea, and cast out there, the Laird of Colzean, whose servant he had been, dreaming of him in his sleep, and that he had a particular mark upon his body, came and took up the body, and found it to be the same person; and caused all that lived near by to come and touch the corpse, as is usual in such cases. All round the place came but Auchindrane and his son, whom nobody suspected, till a young child of his, Mary Muir, seeing the people examined, came in among them; and, when she came near the dead body, it sprang out in bleeding; upon which they were apprehended, and put to the torture."—WODROW's *History*, vol. i. p. 513. The trial of Auchindrane happened in 1611. He was convicted and executed.—HUME's *Criminal Laws*, vol. i. p. 428.[1]

A yet more dreadful case was that of Philip Standfield, tried upon the 30th November, 1687, for cursing his father, (which, by the Scottish law, is a capital crime, *Act* 1661, *chap.* 20,) and for being accessory to his murder. Sir James Standfield, the deceased, was a person of melancholy temperament; so that, when his body was found, in a pond near his own house of Newmilns, he was at first generally supposed to have drowned himself. But the body having been hastily buried, a report arose that he had been strangled by ruffians, instigated by his son Philip, a profligate youth, whom he had disinherited on account of his gross debauchery. Upon this rumour the Privy Council granted warrant to two surgeons of character, named Crawford and Muirhead, to dig up the body, and to report the state in which they should find it. Philip was present on this occasion, and the evidence of both surgeons bears distinctly, that he stood for some time at a distance from the body of his parent; but, being called upon to assist in stretching out the corpse, he put his hand to the head, when the mouth and nostrils instantly gushed with blood. This circumstance, with the evident symptoms of terror and remorse exhibited by young Standfield, seem to have had considerable weight with the jury, and are thus stated in the indictment:—" That his (the deceased's) nearest relations being required to lift the corpse into the coffin, after it had been inspected, upon the said Philip Standfield touching of it, (according to

[1] [See "Auchindrane, or the Ayrshire Tragedy," written by Sir W. Scott, in 1830.—ED.]

God's usual mode of discovering murder,) it bled afresh upon the said Philip; and that thereupon he let the body fall, and fled from it in the greatest consternation, crying, ' Lord have mercy upon me!'" The prisoner was found guilty of being accessory to the murder of his father, although there was little more than strong presumptions against him. It is true, he was at the same time separately convicted of the distinct crimes of having cursed his father, and drunk damnation to the monarchy and hierarchy. His sentence, which was to have his tongue cut out, and hand struck off, previous to his being hanged, was executed with the utmost rigour. He denied the murder with his last breath. "It is," says a contemporary judge, "a dark case of divination, to be remitted to the great day, whether he was guilty or innocent. Only it is certain he was a bad youth, and may serve as a beacon to all profligate persons."—FOUNTAINHALL's *Decisions*, vol. i. 483.

While all ranks believed alike the existence of these prodigies, the vulgar were contented to refer them to the immediate interference of the Deity, or, as they termed it, God's revenge against murder. But those, who, while they had overleaped the bounds of superstition, were still entangled in the mazes of mystic philosophy, amongst whom we must reckon many of the medical practitioners, endeavoured to explain the phenomenon, by referring to the secret power of sympathy, which even Bacon did not venture to dispute. To this occult agency was imputed the cure of wounds, effected by applying salves and powders, not to the wound itself, but to the sword or dagger, by which it had been inflicted; a course of treatment, which, wonderful as it may at first seem, was certainly frequently attended with signal success.[1] This, however, was attributed to magic, and those, who submitted to such a mode of cure, were refused spiritual assistance.

The vulgar continue to believe firmly in the phenomenon of the murdered corpse bleeding at the approach of the murderer. "Many"

[1] The first part of the process was to wash the wound clean, and bind it up so as to promote adhesion, and exclude the air. Now, though the remedies, afterwards applied to the sword, could hardly promote so desirable an issue, yet it is evident the wound stood a good chance of healing by the operation of nature, which, I believe, medical gentlemen call a cure by the first intention.

(I adopt the words of an ingenious correspondent) "are the proofs advanced in confirmation of the opinion, against those who are so hardy as to doubt it; but one, in particular, as it is said to have happened in this place, I cannot help repeating.

"Two young men, going a-fishing in the river Yarrow, fell out; and so high ran the quarrel, that the one, in a passion, stabbed the other to the heart with a fish-spear. Astonished at the rash act, he hesitated whether to fly, give himself up to justice, or conceal the crime; and, in the end, fixed on the latter expedient, burying the body of his friend very deep in the sands. As the meeting had been accidental, he was never suspected, although a visible change was observed in his behaviour, from gaiety to a settled melancholy. Time passed on for the space of fifty years, when a smith, fishing near the same place, discovered an uncommon and curious bone, which he put in his pocket, and afterwards showed to some people in his smithy. The murderer being present, now an old white-headed man, leaning on his staff, desired a sight of the little bone; but how horrible was the issue! no sooner had he touched it than it streamed with purple blood. Being told where it was found, he confessed the crime, was condemned, but was prevented by death from suffering the punishment due to his offence.

"Such opinions, though reason forbids us to believe them, a few moments' reflection on the cause of their origin will teach us to revere. Under the feudal system which prevailed, the rights of humanity were too often violated, and redress very hard to be procured; thus an awful deference to one of the leading attributes of Omnipotence begat on the mind, untutored by philosophy, the first germ of these supernatural effects; which was, by superstitious zeal, assisted, perhaps, by a few instances of sudden remorse, magnified into evidence of indisputable guilt."

THE DÆMON-LOVER.

This ballad, which contains some verses of merit, was taken down from recitation by Mr William Laidlaw, tenant in Traquair-knowe.[1] It contains a legend, which, in various shapes, is current in Scotland. I remember to have heard a ballad, in which a fiend is introduced paying his addresses to a beautiful maiden; but, disconcerted by the holy herbs which she wore in her bosom, makes the following lines the burden of his courtship:—

> "Gin ye wish to be leman mine,
> Lay aside the St John's wort and the vervain."

The heroine of the following tale was unfortunately without any similar protection.

[1] [See a note on the Douglas Tragedy, *antè*.—ED.]

THE DÆMON-LOVER.[1]

"O WHERE have you been, my long, long love,
    This long seven years and more?"—
"O I'm come to seek my former vows
    Ye granted me before."—

"O hold your tongue of your former vows,
    For they will breed sad strife;
O hold your tongue of your former vows,
    For I am become a wife."

He turn'd him right and round about,
    And the tear blinded his ee;
"I wad never hae trodden on Irish ground,
    If it had not been for thee.

"I might hae had a king's daughter,
    Far, far beyond the sea;
I might have had a king's daughter,
    Had it not been for love o' thee."—

[1] ["And woman wailing for her Dæmon-Lover."—COLERIDGE.]

"If ye might have had a king's daughter,
   Yer sell ye had to blame;
Ye might have taken the king's daughter,
   For ye kend that I was nane."—

"O faulse are the vows of womankind,
   But fair is their faulse bodie;
I never wad hae trodden on Irish ground,
   Had it not been for love o' thee."—

"If I was to leave my husband dear,
   And my two babes also,
O what have you to take me to,
   If with you I should go?"—

"I hae seven ships upon the sea,
   The eighth brought me to land;
With four-and-twenty bold mariners,
   And music on every hand."

She has taken up her two little babes,
   Kiss'd them baith cheek and chin;
"O fair ye weel, my ain two babes,
   For I'll never see you again."

She set her foot upon the ship,
   No mariners could she behold;
But the sails were o' the taffetie,
   And the masts o' the beaten gold.

She had not sail'd a league, a league,
    A league but barely three,
When dismal grew his countenance,
    And drumlie[1] grew his ee.

The masts that were like the beaten gold,
    Bent not on the heaving seas;
But the sails, that were o' the taffetie,
    Fill'd not in the east land breeze.

They had not sailed a league, a league,
    A league but barely three,
Until she espied his cloven foot,
    And she wept right bitterlie.

"O hold your tongue of your weeping," says he,
    "Of your weeping now let me be;
I will show you how the lilies grow
    On the banks of Italy."—

"O what hills are yon, yon pleasant hills,
    That the sun shines sweetly on?"—
"O yon are the hills of heaven," he said,
    "Where you will never win."—

"O whaten a mountain is yon," she said,
    "All so dreary wi' frost and snow?"—

[1] *Drumlie*—Clouded; dark.

"O yon is the mountain of hell," he cried,
  "Where you and I will go."

And aye when she turn'd her round about,
  Aye taller he seem'd for to be;
Until that the tops o' that gallant ship
  Nae taller were than he.

The clouds grew dark, and the wind grew loud,
  And the levin fill'd her ee;
And waesome wail'd the snaw-white sprites
  Upon the gurlie sea.

He strack the tap-mast wi' his hand,
  The fore-mast wi' his knee;
And he brake that gallant ship in twain,
  And sank her in the sea.[1]

---

[1] [Mr Motherwell printed, in 1827, some verses of a ruder edition of this ballad (p. 92); and in 1828, Mr Buchan produced a much more extended copy, under the title of "James Herries." See his 1st vol. p. 215. In this edition, the lover is not a dæmon, but the ghost of James Herries, who had been betrothed, before a sea voyage, to "Jeanie Douglas," the heroine.—ED.]

THE
LASS OF LOCHROYAN.

NOW FIRST PUBLISHED IN A PERFECT STATE.

LOCHROYAN, whence this ballad probably derives its name, lies in Galloway. The lover, who, if the story be real, may be supposed to have been detained by sickness, is represented, in the legend, as confined by fairy charms in an enchanted castle situated in the sea. The ruins of ancient edifices are still visible on the summits of most of those small islands, or rather insulated rocks, which lie along the coast of Ayrshire and Galloway; as Ailsa and Big Scaur.

This edition of the ballad is composed of verses selected from three MS. copies, and two obtained from recitation. Two of the copies are in Herd's MS.; the third in that of Mrs Brown of Falkland.

A fragment of the original song, which is sometimes denominated *Lord Gregory*, or *Love Gregory*, was published in Mr Herd's Collection, 1774, and, still more fully, in that of Laurie and Symington, 1792.

The story has been celebrated both by Burns[1] and Dr Wolcott.[2]

[1] ["O mirk, mirk is this midnight hour,
And loud the tempest's roar;
A waefu' wanderer seeks thy tower,
Lord Gregory, ope thy door," &c.
   Cunnin's *Burns*, vol. iv.]

[2] ["Ah! ope, Lord Gregory, thy door,
A midnight wanderer sighs," &c.

Peter Pindar's song was written before Burns's.—Ed.]

THE
LASS OF LOCHROYAN.

"O wha will shoe my bonny foot?
   And wha will glove my hand?
And wha will lace my middle jimp
   Wi' a lang, lang linen band?

"O wha will kame my yellow hair,
   With a new-made silver kame?
And wha will father my young son,
   Till Lord Gregory come hame?"—

"Thy father will shoe thy bonny foot,
   Thy mother will glove thy hand,
Thy sister will lace thy middle jimp,
   Till Lord Gregory come to land.

"Thy brother will kame thy yellow hair
   With a new-made silver kame,
And God will be thy bairn's father
   Till Lord Gregory come hame."—

"But I will get a bonny boat,
　　And I will sail the sea;
And I will gang to Lord Gregory,
　　Since he canna come hame to me."

Syne she's gar'd build a bonny boat,
　　To sail the salt, salt sea;
The sails were o' the light green silk,
　　The tows[1] o' taffety.

She hadna sailed but twenty leagues,
　　But twenty leagues and three,
When she met wi' a rank robber,
　　And a' his company.

"Now whether are ye the queen hersell,
　　(For so ye weel might be,)
Or are ye the Lass of Lochroyan,
　　Seekin' Lord Gregory?"—

"O I am neither the queen," she said,
　　"Nor sic I seem to be;
But I am the Lass of Lochroyan,
　　Seekin' Lord Gregory."—

"O see na thou yon bonny bower,
　　It's a' cover'd o'er wi' tin?

[1] Tows—Ropes.

When thou hast sail'd it round about,
  Lord Gregory is within."

And when she saw the stately tower
  Shining sae clear and bright,
Whilk stood aboon the jawing¹ wave,
  Built on a rock of height;

Says—" Row the boat, my mariners,
  And bring me to the land!
For yonder I see my love's castle
  Close by the salt-sea strand."

She sail'd it round, and sail'd it round,
  And loud, loud cried she—
" Now break, now break, ye fairy charms,
  And set my true love free!"

She's ta'en her young son in her arms,
  And to the door she's gane:
And long she knock'd, and sair she ca'd,
  But answer got she nane.

" O open the door, Lord Gregory!
  O open and let me in!
For the wind blaws through my yellow hair,
  And the rain draps o'er my chin."—

¹ *Jawing*—Dashing.

"Awa, awa, ye ill woman!
　　Ye're no come here for good!
Ye're but some witch or wil warlock,
　　Or mermaid o' the flood."—

"I am neither witch, nor wil warlock,
　　Nor mermaid o' the sea;
But I am Annie of Lochroyan;
　　O open the door to me!"—

"Gin thou be Annie of Lochroyan,
　　(As I trow thou binna she,)
Now tell me some o' the love tokens
　　That past between thee and me."—

"O dinna ye mind, Lord Gregory,
　　As we sat at the wine,
We changed the rings frae our fingers,
　　And I can show thee thine?

"O yours was gude, and gude enough,
　　But aye the best was mine;
For yours was o' the gude red gowd,
　　But mine o' the diamond fine.

"And has na thou mind, Lord Gregory,
　　As we sat on the hill,
Thou twin'd me o' my maidenheid
　　Right sair against my will?

" Now, open the door, Lord Gregory!
   Open the door, I pray!
For thy young son is in my arms,
   And will be dead ere day."—

" If thou be the lass of Lochroyan,
   (As I kenna thou be,)
Tell me some mair o' the love tokens
   Past between me and thee."

Fair Annie turn'd her round about—
   " Weel! since that it be sae,
May never a woman that has borne a son,
   Hae a heart sae fou o' wae!

" Take down, take down, that mast o' gowd!
   Set up a mast o' tree!
It disna become a forsaken lady
   To sail sae royallie."

When the cock had crawn, and the day did dawn,
   And the sun began to peep,
Then up and raise him Lord Gregory,
   And sair, sair did he weep.

" Oh I hae dream'd a dream, mother,
   I wish it may prove true!
That the bonny Lass of Lochroyan
   Was at the yate e'en now.

"O I hae dream'd a dream, mother,
  The thought o't gars me greet!
That fair Annie o' Lochroyan
  Lay cauld dead at my feet."—

"Gin it be for Annie of Lochroyan
  That ye make a' this din,
She stood a' last night at your door,
  But I true she wan na in."—

"O wae betide ye, ill woman!
  An ill deid may ye die!
That wadna open the door to her,
  Nor yet wad waken me."

O he's gane down to yon shore side
  As fast as he could fare;
He saw fair Annie in the boat,
  But the wind it toss'd her sair.

"And hey, Annie, and how, Annie!
  O Annie, winna ye bide!"
But aye the mair he cried Annie,
  The braider grew the tide.

"And hey, Annie, and how, Annie!
  Dear Annie, speak to me!"
But aye the louder he cried Annie,
  The louder roar'd the sea.

The wind blew loud, the sea grew rough,
　　And dash'd the boat on shore;
Fair Annie floated through the faem,
　　But the babie rose no more.

Lord Gregory tore his yellow hair,
　　And made a heavy moan;
Fair Annie's corpse lay at his feet,
　　Her bonny young son was gone.

O cherry, cherry was her cheek,
　　And gowden was her hair;
But clay-cold were her rosy lips—
　　Nae spark o' life was there.

And first he kiss'd her cherry cheek,
　　And syne he kiss'd her chin,
And syne he kiss'd her rosy lips—
　　There was nae breath within.

" O wae betide my cruel mother!
　　An ill death may she die!
She turn'd my true love frae my door,
　　Wha came sae far to me.

" O wae betide my cruel mother!
　　An ill death may she die!
She turn'd fair Annie frae my door,
　　Wha died for love o' me."

ROSE THE RED AND WHITE LILLY.

NEVER BEFORE PUBLISHED.

This legendary tale is given chiefly from Mrs BROWN's *MS. Accordingly, many of the rhymes arise from the northern mode of pronunciation; as* dee *for* do, *and the like.—Perhaps the ballad may have originally related to the history of the celebrated* ROBIN HOOD, *as mention is made of Barnisdale, his favourite abode.*[1]

O ROSE the Red, and White Lilly,
   Their mother deir was dead;
And their father has married an ill woman,
   Wish'd them twa little guid.

---

[1] [Mr Kinloch has published (*Ancient Ballads*, 1827, p. 69) a curious ballad, entitled, " The Wedding of Robin Hood and Little John," which had not before appeared in print; and which sustains Sir Walter Scott's conjecture as to the true hero of " Rose the Red and White Lilly." In Mr Buchan's edition of " Rose the Red," &c., printed in 1828, the name of Robin Hood occurs also; but this is only a vulgarized and mean transformation of the ballad in the text.—ED.]

But she had twa as gallant sons
    As ever brake man's bread;
And the tane o' them lo'ed her, White Lilly,
    And the tother Rose the Red.

O bigged hae they a bigly bour,
    Fast by the roaring strand;
And there was mair mirth in the ladyes' bour,
    Nor in a' their father's land.

But out and spak their step-mother,
    As she stood a little forbye—
" I hope to live and play the prank,
    Sall gar your loud sang lie."

She's call'd upon her eldest son;
    " Cum here, my son, to me:
It fears me sair, my Bauld Arthur,
    That ye maun sail the sea."—

" Gin sae it maun be, my deir mother,
    Your bidding I maun dee;
But be never waur to Rose the Red,
    Than ye hae been to me."

She's call'd upon her youngest son;
    " Cum here, my son, to me:

It fears me sair, my Brown Robin,
    That ye maun sail the sea."—

"Gin it fear ye sair, my mother deir,
    Your bidding I sall dee;
But, be never waur to White Lilly,
    Than ye hae been to me."—

"Now haud your tongues, ye foolish boys!
    For small sall be their part:
They ne'er again sall see your face,
    Gin their very hearts suld break."

Sae Bauld Arthur's gane to our King's court,
    His hie chamberlain to be;
But Brown Robin, he has slain a knight,
    And to grene-wood he did flee.

When Rose the Red, and White Lilly,
    Saw their twa loves were gane,
Sune did they drop the loud, loud sang,
    Took up the still mourning.

And out then spake her White Lilly;
    "My sister, we'll be gane:
Why suld we stay in Barnisdale,
    To mourn our bour within?"

O cutted hae they their green cloathing,
    A little abune their knee;

And sae hae they their yellow hair,
  A little abune their bree."[1]

And left hae they that bonny bour,
  To cross the raging sea;
And they hae ta'en to a holy chapel,
  Was christened by Our Ladye.

And they hae changed their twa names,
  Sae far frae ony toun;
And the tane o' them's hight Sweet Willie,
  And the tother's Rouge the Rounde.

Between the twa a promise is,
  And they hae sworn it to fulfil;
Whenever the tane blew a bugle-horn,
  The tother suld cum her till.

Sweet Willy's gane to the King's court,
  Her true love for to see;
And Rouge the Rounde to gude grene-wood,
  Brown Robin's man to be.

O it fell anes, upon a tyme,
  They putted at the stane;

[1] [" And they hae kilt their gay claithing
A little below their knee—
And they are on in gude greenwood,
Gif Robin Hood they see."—KINLOCH, p. 71.]

And seven foot ayont them a',
    Brown Robin's gar'd it gang.

She lifted the heavy putting-stane,
    And gave a sad " O hon!"
Then out bespake him, Brown Robin,
    " But that's a woman's moan!"—

" O kent ye by my rosy lips?
    Or by my yellow hair?
Or kent ye by my milk-white breast,
    Ye never yet saw bare?"—

" I kent na by your rosy lips,
    Nor by your yellow hair;
But, cum to your bour whaever likes,
    They'll find a ladye there."—[1]

" O gin ye cum my bour within,
    Through fraud, deceit, or guile;
Wi' this same brand, that's in my hand,
    I vow I will thee kill."—

---

[1] [" Then up bespak him Robin Hood,
    As he to them drew near,
' Instead of boys to carry the bows,
    Two ladies we've got here.' "—KINLOCH, p. 72.
The *next* verse is:—
    " So they had not been in gude green-wood,
        A twalmonth and a day,
    Till Rogie Roun was as big wi' bairn,
        As ony lady could gae."—ED.]

"Yet durst I cum into your bour,
　And ask nae leave," quo' he;
"And wi' this same brand, that's in my hand,
　Wave danger back on thee."

About the dead hour o' the night,
　The ladye's bour was broken;
And, about the first hour o' the day,
　The fair knave bairn was gotten.

When days were gane and months were come,
　The ladye was sad and wan;
And aye she cried for a bour woman,
　For to wait her upon.

Then up and spake him, Brown Robin,
　"And what needs this?" quo' he;
"Or what can woman do for you,
　That canna be done by me?"—

"'Twas never my mother's fashion," she said,
　"Nor shall it e'er be mine,
That belted knights should e'er remain
　While ladyes dree'd their pain.

"But gin ye take that bugle-horn,
　And wind a blast sae shrill,
I hae a brother in yonder court
　Will come me quickly till."—

"O gin ye hae a brother on earth,
   That ye lo'e mair than me,
Ye may blow the horn yoursell," he says,
   "For a blast I winna gie."

She's ta'en the bugle in her hand,
   And blawn baith loud and shrill;
Sweet William started at the sound,
   And came her quickly till.

O up and starts him, Brown Robin,
   And swore by Our Ladye,
"No man shall come into this bour,
   But first maun fight wi' me."

O they hae fought the wood within,
   Till the sun was going down;
And drops o' blood, frae Rose the Red,
   Came pouring to the ground.

She leant her back against an aik,
   Said—"Robin, let me be;
For it is a ladye, bred and born,
   That has fought this day wi' thee."

O seven foot he started back,
   Cried—"Alas and woe is me!
For I wished never, in all my life,
   A woman's bluid to see:

" And that all for the knightly vow
   I swore to Our Ladye :
But mair for the sake o' ae fair maid,
   Whose name was White Lilly."

Then out and spake her, Rouge the Rounde,
   And leugh right hertilie,
" She has been wi' ye this year and mair,
   Though ye wistna it was she."

Now word is gane through all the land,
   Before a month was gane,
That a forester's page, in gude grene-wood,
   Had born a bonny son.

The marvel gaed to the King's court,
   And to the King himsell ;
" Now, by my fae," the King did say,
   " The like was never heard tell ! "

Then out and spake him, Bauld Arthur,
   And laugh'd right loud and hie—
" I trow some may has plaid the lown,[1]
   And fled her ain countrie."—

" Bring me my steid ! " the King can say ;
   " My bow and arrows keen ;

[1] *Lown*—Rogue.

And I'll gae hunt in yonder wood,
 And see what's to be seen."—

"Gin it please your grace," quo' Bauld Arthur,
 " My liege, I'll gang you wi',
And see gin I can meet a bonny page,
 That's stray'd awa frae me."

And they hae chased in gude grene-wood,
 The buck but and the rae,
Till they drew near Brown Robin's bour,
 About the close o' day.

Then out an' spake the King himsell,
 Says—" Arthur, look and see,
Gin yon be not your favourite page,
 That leans against yon tree."

O Arthur's ta'en a bugle-horn,
 And blawn a blast sae shrill;
Sweet Willie started to her feet,
 And ran him quickly till.

" O wanted ye your meat, Willie,
 Or wanted ye your fee?
Or gat ye e'er an angry word,
 That ye ran awa frae me?"—

"I wanted nought, my master dear;
　　To me ye aye was good:
I cam to see my ae brother,
　　That wons in this grene-wood."

Then out bespake the King again,—
　　"My boy, now tell to me,
Who dwells into yon bigly bour,
　　Beneath yon green aik tree?"—

"O pardon me," said Sweet Willy,
　　"My liege, I darena tell;
And gangna near yon Outlaw's bour,
　　For fear they suld you kill."—

"O haud your tongue, my bonny boy!
　　For I winna be said nay;
But I will gang yon bour within,
　　Betide me weal or wae."

They have lighted frae their milk-white steids,
　　And saftlie entered in;
And there they saw her, White Lilly,
　　Nursing her bonny young son.

"Now, by the mass," the King he said,
　　"This is a comely sight;
I trow, instead of a forester's man,
　　This is a ladye bright!"

O out and spake her, Rose the Red,
   And fell low on her knee :—
" O pardon us, my gracious liege,
   And our story I'll tell thee.

" Our father is a wealthy lord,
   Lives into Barnisdale ;
But we had a wicked step-mother,
   That wrought us meikle bale.

" Yet had she twa as fu' fair sons,
   As e'er the sun did see ;
And the tane o' them lo'ed my sister deir,
   And the tother said he lo'ed me."—

Then out and cried him, Bauld Arthur,
   As by the King he stood,—
" Now, by the faith of my body,
   This suld be Rose the Red!"

The King has sent for robes o' green,
   And girdles o' shining gold ;
And sae sune have the ladyes busked themselves,
   Sae glorious to behold.

Then in and came him, Brown Robin,
   Frae hunting o' the King's deer,
But when he saw the King himsell,
   He started back for fear.

The King has ta'en Robin by the hand,
 And bade him nothing dread,
But quit for aye the gude grene-wood,
 And come to the court wi' speed.

The King has ta'en White Lilly's son,
 And set him on his knee;
Says—" Gin ye live to wield a brand,
 My bowman thou sall be."

Then they have ta'en them to the holy chapelle,
 And there had fair wedding;
And when they cam to the King's court,
 For joy the bells did ring.[1]

[1] [The ballad in Kinloch ends thus:
 " The tane was wedded to Robin Hood,
  And the other to Little John;
  And it was a' owing to their stepmother
   That garr'd them leave their hame "—P. 73.—ED.]

FAUSE FOODRAGE.

NEVER BEFORE PUBLISHED.

This ballad has been popular in many parts of Scotland. It is chiefly given from Mrs Brown of Falkland's MSS.—The expression,

"The boy stared wild like a gray goss-hawk," *Verse* 31,

strongly resembles that in *Hardyknute*,

"Norse e'en like gray goss-hawk stared wild;"

a circumstance which led the Editor to make the strictest enquiry into the authenticity of the song. But every doubt was removed by the evidence of a lady of high rank,[1] who not only recollected the ballad, as having amused her infancy, but could repeat many of the verses, particularly those beautiful stanzas from the 20th to the 25th. The Editor is therefore compelled to believe, that the author of *Hardyknute* copied the old ballad; if the coincidence be not 'altogether accidental.

[1] [The late Lady Douglas of Douglas, sister to Henry Duke of Buccleuch.—Ed.]

The *King Easter* and *King Wester* of the ballad were probably petty princes of Northumberland and Westmoreland. In the *Complaynt of Scotland*, an ancient romance is mentioned, under the title, " *How the King of Estmureland married the King's daughter of Westmureland,*" which may possibly be the original of the beautiful legend of *King Estmere*, in the *Reliques of Ancient English Poetry*, vol. i. p. 62, 4th edit.[1] From this it may be conjectured, with some degree of plausibility, that the independent kingdoms of the east and west coast were, at an early period, thus denominated, according to the Saxon mode of naming districts from their relative positions, as Essex, Wessex, Sussex. But the geography of the metrical romances sets all system at defiance; and, in some of these, as *Clariodus and Meliades*, Estmureland undoubtedly signifies the land of the Easterlings, or the Flemish provinces at which vessels arrived in three days from England, and to which they are represented as exporting wool.— *Vide Notes on Kempion*, (p. 241, post.)

[1] On this subject I have, since publication of the first edition, been favoured with the following remarks by Mr Ritson, in opposition to the opinion above expressed:—

" Estmureland and Westmureland have no sort of relation to Northumberland and Westmoreland. The former was never called Eastmoreland, nor were there ever any kings of Westmoreland; unless we admit the authority of an old rhyme, cited by Usher :—

' Here the King Westmer
Slew the King Rothinger.'

"There is, likewise, a 'King Estmere of Spain,' in one of Percy's ballads.

"In the old metrical romance of *Kyng Horn*, or *Horn Child*, we find both Westnesse and Estnesse; and it is somewhat singular, that two places, so called, actually exist in Yorkshire at this day. But *ness*, in that quarter, is the name given to an inlet from a river. There is, however, great confusion in this poem, as *Horn* is called king sometimes of one country, and sometimes of the other. In the French original, Westir is said to have been the old name of Hirland or Irvland; which, occasionally at least, is called Westnesse, in the translation, in which Britain is named Sudene; but here, again, it is inconsistent and confused.

"It is, at any rate, highly probable, that the story, cited in the *Complaynt of Scotland*, was a romance of *King Horn*, whether prose or verse; and, consequently, that Estmureland and Westmureland should there mean England and Ireland; though it is possible that no other instance can be found of these two names occurring with the same sense."

FAUSE FOODRAGE.

King Easter has courted her for her lands,
  King Wester for her fee,
King Honour for her comely face,
  And for her fair bodie.

They had not been four months married,
  As I have heard them tell,
Until the nobles of the land
  Against them did rebel.

And they cast kevils[1] them amang,
  And kevils them between;
And they cast kevils them amang,
  Wha suld gae kill the king.

---

[1] *Kevils*—Lots. Both words originally meant only a portion, or share of any thing.—*Leges Burgorum*, cap. 59, *de lot, cut, or kavil. Statuta Gildæ*, cap. 20. *Nullus emat lanam, &c. nisi fuerit confrater Gildæ, &c. Neque* lot *neque* cavil *habeat cum aliquo confratre nostro.* In both these laws, *lot* and *cavil* signify a share in trade.

O, some said yea, and some said nay,
    Their words did not agree;
Till up and got him, Fause Foodrage,
    And swore it suld be he.

When bells were rung, and mass was sung,
    And a' men bound to bed,
King Honour and his gay ladye
    In a high chamber were laid.

Then up and raise him, Fause Foodrage,
    When a' were fast asleep,
And slew the porter in his lodge,
    That watch and ward did keep.

O four and twenty silver keys
    Hang hie upon a pin;
And aye, as ae door he did unlock,
    He has fasten'd it him behind.

Then up and raise him, King Honour,
    Says—" What means a' this din?
Or what's the matter, Fause Foodrage,
    Or wha has loot you in?"—

" O ye my errand weel sall learn,
    Before that I depart."—
Then drew a knife, baith lang and sharp,
    And pierced him to the heart.

Then up and got the Queen hersell,
    And fell low down on her knee
" O spare my life, now, Fause Foodrage!
    For I never injured thee.

" O spare my life, now, Fause Foodrage!
    Until I lighter be!
And see gin it be lad or lass,
    King Honour has left me wi'."—

" O gin it be a lass," he says,
    " Weel nursed it sall be ;
But gin it be a lad bairn,
    He sall be hanged hie.

" I winna spare for his tender age,
    Nor yet for his hie hie kin ;
But soon as e'er he born is,
    He sall mount the gallows pin."—

O four-and-twenty valiant knights
    Were set the Queen to guard ;
And four stood aye at her bour door,
    To keep both watch and ward.

But when the time drew near an end,
    That she suld lighter be,
She cast about to find a wile,
    To set her body free.

O she has birled these merry young men
    With the ale but and the wine,
Until they were a' deadly drunk
    As any wild-wood swine.

" O narrow, narrow is this window,
    And big, big am I grown!"—
Yet through the might of Our Ladye,
    Out at it she is gone.

She wander'd up, she wander'd down,
    She wander'd out and in;
And, at last, into the very swine's stythe,
    The Queen brought forth a son.

Then they cast kevils them amang,
    Which suld gae seek the Queen;
And the kevil fell upon Wise William,
    And he sent his wife for him.

O when she saw Wise William's wife,
    The Queen fell on her knee:
" Win up, win up, madam!" she says:
    " What needs this courtesie?"—

" O out o' this I winna rise,
    Till a boon ye grant to me;
To change your lass for this lad bairn,
    King Honour left me wi'.

" And ye maun learn my gay goss-hawk
    Right weel to breast a steed ;
And I sall learn your turtle dow¹
    As weel to write and read.

" And ye maun learn my gay goss-hawk
    To wield both bow and brand ;
And I sall learn your turtle dow
    To lay gowd² wi' her hand.

" At kirk and market when we meet,
    We'll dare make nae avowe,
But—' Dame, how does my gay goss-hawk ?'³
    ' Madame, how does my dow ?'"

¹ *Dow*—Dove.
² *Lay gowd*—To embroider in gold.
³ This metaphorical language was customary among the northern nations. In 925, King Adelstein sent an embassy to Harald Harfager, King of Norway, the chief of which presented that prince with an elegant sword, ornamented with precious stones. As it was presented by the point, the Norwegian chief, in receiving it, unwarily laid hold of the hilt. The English ambassador declared, in the name of his master, that he accepted the act as a deed of homage ; for touching the hilt of a warrior's sword was regarded as an acknowledgment of subjection. The Norwegian prince, resolving to circumvent his rival by a similar artifice, suppressed his resentment, and sent, next summer, an embassy to Adelstein, the chief of which presented Haco, the son of Harald, to the English prince ; and, placing him on his knees, made the following declaration :—" *Haraldus, Normanorum Rex, amice te salutat ; albamque hanc avem bene institutam mittit, atque melius deinceps*

When days were gane, and years came on,
    Wise William he thought lang;
And he has ta'en King Honour's son
    A-hunting for to gang.

It sae fell out, at this hunting,
    Upon a simmer's day,
That they came by a fair castell,
    Stood on a sunny brae.

" O dinna ye see that bonny castell,
    Wi' halls and towers sae fair?
Gin ilka man had back his ain,
    Of it you suld be heir."—

" How I suld be heir of that castell,
    In sooth, I canna see;
For it belangs to Fause Foodrage,
    And he is na kin to me."—

" O gin ye suld kill him, Fause Foodrage,
    You would do but what was right;
For I wot he kill'd your father dear,
    Or ever ye saw the light.

erudias, postulat." The king received young Haco on his knees; which the Norwegian ambassador immediately accepted, in the name of his master, as a declaration of inferiority; according to the proverb, " *Is minor semper habetur, qui alterius filium educat.*"—Pontoppidani Vestigia Danor., vol. ii. p. 67.

" And gin ye suld kill him, Fause Foodrage,
   There is no man durst you blame;
For he keeps your mother a prisoner,
   And she darna take ye hame."—

The boy stared wild like a gray goss-hawk;
   Says—" What may a' this mean ? "—
" My boy, ye are King Honour's son,
   And your mother's our lawful Queen."—

" O gin I be King Honour's son,
   By Our Ladye I swear,
This night I will that traitor slay,
   And relieve my mother dear ! "—

He has set his bent bow to his breast,
   And leaped the castell wa';
And soon he has seized on Fause Foodrage,
   Wha loud for help 'gan ca'.

" O haud your tongue, now, Fause Foodrage,
   Frae me ye shanna flee ; "—
Syne pierced him through the fause, fause heart,
   And set his mother free.

And he has rewarded Wise William,
   Wi' the best half of his land ;
And sae has he the turtle dow,
   Wi' the truth o' his right hand.

KEMPION.

NEVER BEFORE PUBLISHED.

The tale of *Kempion* seems, from the names of the personages, and the nature of the adventure, to have been an old metrical romance, degraded into a ballad, by the lapse of time, and the corruption of reciters. The change in the structure of the last verses, from the common ballad stanzas, to that which is proper to the metrical romance, adds force to this conjecture.

Such transformations, as the song narrates, are common in the annals of chivalry. In the 25th and 26th cantos of the second book of the *Orlando Inamorato*, the Paladin, *Brandimarte*, after surmounting many obstacles, penetrates into the recesses of an enchanted palace. Here he finds a fair damsel, seated upon a tomb, who announces to him, that, in order to achieve her deliverance, he must raise the lid of the sepulchre, and kiss whatever being should issue forth. The knight, having pledged his faith, proceeds to open the tomb, out of which a monstrous snake issues forth, with a tremendous hiss. *Brandimarte*, with much reluctance, fulfils the *bizarre* conditions of the adventure;

and the monster is instantly changed into a beautiful
Fairy, who loads her deliverer with benefits. For the
satisfaction of those who may wish to compare the tale
of the Italian Poet with that of *Kempion*, a part of the
original of Boiardo is given below.[1]

[1] Poich' ebbe il verso Brandimarte letto,
La lapida pesante in aria alzava:
Ecco fuor una serpe insin' al petto,
La qual, forte stridendo, zufolava,
Di spaventoso, e terribil' aspetto,
Aprendo il muso gran denti mostrava,
De' quali il cavalier non si fidando,
Si trasse a dietro, et misse mano al brando.

Ma quella Donna gridava "non fate"
Col viso smorto, a grido tremebondo,
"Non far, che ci farai periculare,
E cadrem' tutti quanti nel profondo;
A te convien quella serpe baciare,
O far pensier di non esser' al mondo,
Accostar la tua bocca con la sua,
O perduta tener la vita tua."

"Come! non vedi, che i denti degrigna,
Che pajon fatti a posta a spiccar' nasi,
E fammi un certo viso de matrigna,"
Disse il Guerrier, "ch'io me spavento quasi?"
"Anzi t' invita con faccia benigna,"
Disse la Donna, "e molti altri rimasi
Per viltà sono a questa sepoltura;
Or la t' accosta, e non aver paura."

Il cavalier s' accosta, ma di passo,
Che troppo grato quel baciar non gli era,
Verso la serpe chinandosi basso,

There is a ballad, somewhat resembling *Kempion*, called the *Laidley Worm of Spindleston-heugh*, which is very popular upon the Borders; but having been often published, it was thought unnecessary to insert

Gli parvo tanto orrenda, e tanto fera,
Che venne in viso freddo, com' un sasso;
E disse "si fortuna vuol' ch'io pera,
Fia tanto un altra volta, quanto addesso
Ma cagion dar non me ne voglio io stesso.

"Fuss' io certo d'andare in paradiso,
Come son' certo, chinandomi un poco,
Che quella bestia mi s'avventa al viso,
E mi piglia nel naso, o altro loco:
Egli e proprio così, com' io m'avviso,
Ch' altri ch'io stato e colto a questo gioco,
E che costei mi da questo conforto
Per vindicarsi di colui, ch'ho morto."[1]

Così discendo, a rinculare attende,
Deliberato più non s'accostare:
La donna si dispera, e lo reprende,
"Ah codardo," dicea, "che credi fare?
Perche tanta viltà l'alma t'offende,
Che ti farà alla fin mal capitare?
Infinita paura e poca fede,
La salute gli mostro, e non mi crede."

Punto il Guerrier de questi agre parole,
Torna di nuovo ver la sepoltura,
Tinsegli in rose il color di viole,
In vergogna mutata la paura:
Pur stando ancor' fra due, vuole, e non vuole,

[1] Un cavalier ucciso per Brandimarte nel entrare del palazzo incantato.

it in this collection. The most common version was
either entirely composed, or rewritten, by the Reverend
Mr Lamb, of Norham.

A similar tradition is, by Heywood and Deliro, said
to have existed at Basil. A tailor, in an adventurous
mood, chose to descend into an obscure cavern, in the
vicinity of the city. After many windings he came to
an iron door, through which he passed into a splendid
chamber. Here he found, seated upon a stately throne,
a lady, whose countenance was surprisingly beautiful,
but whose shape terminated in a dragon's train, which
warped around the chair on which she was placed.
Before her stood a brazen chest, trebly barred and
bolted; at each end of which lay couched a huge black
ban-dog, who rose up, as if to tear the intruder in
pieces. But the lady appeased them; and, opening the
chest, displayed an immense treasure, out of which she
bestowed upon the visitor some small pieces of money,
informing him, that she was enchanted by her step-

> Un pensier lo spaventa, un l'assicura,
> Al fin tra l'animoso, e'l disperato,
> A lei s'accosta, ed halle un bacio dato.
>
> Un ghiaccio proprio gli parne a toccare
> La bocca, che parea prima di foco:
> La serpe se commincia a tramutare,
> E diventa donzella a poco a poco:
> Febosilla costei si fa chiamare,
> Una fata, che fece quel bel loco,
> E quel giardino, e quella sepoltura,
> Ove gran tempo e stato in pena dura, &c.

dame, but should recover her natural shape on being kissed thrice by a mortal. The tailor essayed to fulfil the conditions of the adventure; but her face assumed such an altered, wild, and grim expression, that his courage failed, and he was fain to fly from the place. A kinsman of his, some years after, penetrated into the cavern, with the purpose of repairing a desperate fortune. But, finding nothing but dead men's bones, he ran mad and died. Sir John Mandeville tells a similar story of a Grecian island.

There are numerous traditions upon the Borders, concerning huge and destructive snakes, and also of a poisonous reptile called a *man-keeper;* although the common adder, and blind worm, are the only reptiles of that *genus* now known to haunt our wilds. Whether it be possible, that, at an early period, before the country was drained, and cleared of wood, serpents of a larger size may have existed, is a question which the Editor leaves to the naturalist. But, not to mention the fabulous dragon, slain in Northumberland by *Sir Bevis*, the fame still survives of many a *preux chevalier*, supposed to have distinguished himself by similar achievements.

The manor of Sockburne, in the bishopric of Durham, anciently the seat of the family of Conyers, or Cogniers, is held of the bishop by the service of presenting, or showing to him, upon his first entrance into his diocese, an antique sword, or falchion. The origin of this peculiar service is thus stated in Beckwith's edition of BLOUNT's *Ancient Tenures*, p. 200.

"Sir Edward Blackett (the proprietor of the manor) now represents the person of Sir John Conyers, who, as tradition says, in the fields of Sockburne, slew, with his falchion, a monstrous creature, a dragon, a worm, or flying serpent, that devoured men, women, and children. The then owner of Sockburne, as a reward for his bravery, gave him the manor, with its appurtenances, to hold for ever, on condition that he meets the Lord Bishop of Durham, with this falchion, on his first entrance into his diocese, after his election to that see.

"And, in confirmation of this tradition, there is painted, in a window of Sockburne church, the falchion we just now spoke of: and it is also cut in marble, upon the tomb of the great ancestor of the Conyers', together with a dog, and the monstrous worm, or serpent, lying at his feet, of his own killing, of which the history of the family gives the above account.

"When the Bishop first comes into his diocese, he crosses the river Tees, either at the ford of Nesham, or Croft-Bridge, where the counties of York and Durham divide; at one of which places Sir Edward Blackett, either in person, or by his representative, if the Bishop comes by Nesham, rides into the middle of the river Tees, with the ancient falchion drawn in his hand, or upon the middle of Croft-Bridge; and then presents the falchion to the Bishop, addressing him in the ancient form of words: upon which the Bishop takes the falchion into his hand, looks at it, and returns it back again, wishing the lord of the manor his health, and the enjoyment of his estate." The falchion above alluded to has upon its hilt the arms of England, in the reign of King John, and an eagle, supposed to be the ensign of Morcar, Earl of Northumberland.—Gough's *Camden's Britannia*, vol. iii. p. 114. Mr Gough, with great appearance of probability, conjectures the dragon, engraved on the tomb, to be an emblematical, or heraldic ornament.

The property, called Pollard's Lands, near Bishop Auckland, is held by a similar tenure; and we are informed, in the work just quoted, that " Dr Johnson of Newcastle met the present Bishop, Dr Egerton, in September, 1771, at his first arrival there, and presented a falchion upon his knee, and addressed him in the old form of words, saying, *My lord, in behalf of myself, as well as of the several other tenants of Pollard's Lands, I do humbly present your lordship with this falchion, at your first coming here, wherewith, as the tradition goeth, Pollard slew of old a great and venomous serpent, which did much harm to man and beast: and by the performance of this service these lands are holden.*"—Ancient Tenures, p. 201.

Above the south entrance of the ancient parish church of Linton, in Roxburghshire, is a rude piece of sculpture, representing a knight, with a falcon on his arm, encountering with his lance, in full career, a sort of monster, which the common people call a *worm*, or snake. Tradition bears, that this animal inhabited a den, or hollow, at some distance from the church, whence it was wont to issue forth, and ravage the country, or, by the fascination of its eyes and breath, draw its prey into its jaws. Large rewards were in vain offered for the destruction of this monster, which had grown to so huge a bulk, that it used to twist itself, in spiral folds, round a green hillock of considerable height, still called Wormeston, and marked by a clump of trees. When sleeping in this place, with its mouth open, popular credulity affirms, that it was slain by the Laird of Lariston, a man brave even to madness, who, coming upon the snake at full gallop, thrust down its throat a *peat* (a piece of turf dried for fuel) dipt in scalding pitch, and fixed to the point of his lance. The aromatic quality of the peat is said to have preserved the champion from the effects of the monster's poisonous breath, while, at the same time, it clogged its jaws. In dying, the serpent contracted its folds with so much violence, that their spiral impression is still discernible round the hillock where it lay. The noble family of Somerville are said to bo descended from this adventurous knight, in memory of whose achievement they bear a dragon as their crest.

The sculpture itself gives no countenance to this fine story; for the animal, whom the knight appears to be in the act of slaying, has no resemblance to a serpent, but rather to a wolf, or boar, with which the neighbouring Cheviot mountains must in early times have abounded;[1] and there remain vestiges of another monster, of the same species, attacking the horse of the champion. An inscription, which might have thrown light upon this exploit, is now totally defaced. The vulgar adapting it to their own tradition, tell us that it ran thus:

> " The wode Laird af Lariestoun
> Slew the wode worm of Wormiestoune,
> And wan all Lintoun parochine."

It is most probable, that the animal destroyed by the ancestor of Lord Somerville, was one of those beasts of prey by which Caledonia was formerly infested, but which, now,

> " Razed out of all her woods, as trophies hung,
> Grin high emblazon'd on her children's shields."

Since publishing the first edition of this work I have found the following account of Somerville's achievement, in a MS. of some antiquity:—

" John Somerville (son to Roger de Somerville, baron of Wichenever, in Staffordshire) was made, by King William (the lion), his principal falconer, and got from that King the lands and baronie of Linton, in

---

[1] An altar, dedicated to Sylvan Mars, was found in a glen in Weardale, in the bishopric of Durham. From the following votive inscription, it appears to have been erected by C. T. V. Micianus, a Roman general, upon taking an immense boar, which none of his predecessors could destroy:

" Silvano invicto sacrum, C. Tetius Veturius Miclanus Præf. Alæ Sebosinæ ob aprum eximiæ formæ captum, quem multi ante-

Teviotdale, for an extraordinarie and valiant action, which, according to the manuscript of the family of Drum, was thus: In the parochen of Lintoun, within the sheriffdom of Roxburgh, there happened to breed a monster, in form of a serpent or worme; in length, three Scots yards, and somewhat bigger than an ordinarie man's leg, with a head more proportionable to its length than greatnesse. It had its den in a hollow piece of ground, a mile south-east from Lintoun church; it destroyed both men and beasts that came in its way. Several attempts were made to destroy it, by shooting of arrows, and throwing of darts, none daring to approach so near as to make use of a sword or lance. John Somerville undertakes to kill it, and being well mounted, and attended with a stoute servant, he cam, before the sun-rising, before the dragon's den, having prepared some long, small, and hard peats (bog-turf dried for fuel,) bedubbed with pitch, rosett, and brimstone, fixed with a small wire upon a wheel, at the point of his lance; these, being touched with fire, would instantly break out into flames; and, there being a breath of air, that served to his purpose, about the sun-rising, the serpent, dragon, or worme, so called by tradition, appeared with her head, and some part of her body, without the den; whereupon his servant set fire to the peats upon the wheel, at the top of the lance, and John Somerville, advancing with a full gallop, thrust

ænsores ejus prædari non potuerunt, Votum solvens lubenter posuit."—LAMB's Notes on Battle of Flodden, 1774, p. 67.

the same with the wheel, and a great part of the lance, directly into the serpent's mouth, which wente down its throat into the belly, and was left there, the lance breaking by the rebounding of the horse, and giving a deadly wound to the dragon; for which actione he was knighted by King William; and his effigies was cut in ston in the posture he performed this actione, and placed above the principal church door of Lintoun, where it is yet to be seen, with his name and sirname: and the place, where this monster was killed, is at this day called, by the common people, who have the foresaid story by tradition, the Wormes Glen. And further to perpetuate this actione, the barons of Lintoun, Cowthally, and Drum, did always carry for crest, a wheel, and thereon a dragon."—Extracted from a genealogical MS. in the Advocates' Library, written about 1680. The falcon on the champion's arm, in the monument, may be supposed to allude to his office of falconer to William of Scotland.

The ballad of *Kempion* is given chiefly from Mrs Brown's MS., with corrections from a recited fragment.[1]

---

[1] [Mr Motherwell has printed from recitation, in the west of Scotland, a version of this ballad, in which, he thinks, the name of the hero is given " in greater purity than in any before published." " *Kemp Owayne*," he says, " is no doubt the same Ewain or Owain ap Urien, King of Reged, (i. e. Strathclyde,) who is celebrated by Taliesin and Llywarch-hen, and also in the Welsh Triads." *Kemp* means hero, or *champion*. The other various readings in Mr Motherwell's copy are unimportant.—ED.]

KEMPION.

"Cum heir, cum heir, ye freely feed,
  And lay your head low on my knee;
The heaviest weird[1] I will you read,
  That ever was read to gay ladye.

"O meikle dolour sall ye dree,
  And aye the salt seas o'er ye'se swim;
And far mair dolour sall ye dree
  On Estmere crags,[2] when ye them climb.

"I weird ye to a fiery beast,[3]
  And relieved sall ye never be,

---

[1] *Weird*—From the German auxiliary verb *werden*, "to become."

[2] If by *Estmere Crags* we are to understand the rocky cliffs of Northumberland, in opposition to Westmoreland, we may bring our scene of action near Bamborough, and thereby almost identify the tale of *Kempion* with that of the *Laidley Worm of Spindleston*, to which it bears so strong a resemblance.

[3] Our ideas of dragons and serpents are probably derived from the Scandinavians. The legends of *Regnar Lodbrog*, and of the huge snake in the Edda, by whose folds the world is encircled, are well known. Griffins and dragons were fabled by the Danes, as watching over and defending hoards of gold.—*Bartholin. de caus.*

Till Kempion, the kingis son,
  Cum to the crag, and thrice kiss thee."—

O meikle dolour did she dree,
  And aye the salt seas o'er she swam;
And far mair dolour did she dree
  On Estmere crags, when she them clamb.

And aye she cried for Kempion,
  Gin he would but come to her hand:
Now word has gane to Kempion,
  That sicken a beast was in his land.

" Now, by my sooth," said Kempion,
  " This fiery beast I'll gang and see."—
" And by my sooth," said Segramour,
  " My ae brother, I'll gang wi' thee."

Then bigged hae they a bonny boat,
  And they hae set her to the sea;
But a mile before they reach'd the shore,
  Around them she gar'd the red fire flee.

Cont. mortis, p. 490. *Saxo Grammaticus*, lib. 2. The Edda also mentions one Fafner, who, transformed into a serpent, brooded over his hidden treasures. From these authorities, and that of Herodotus, our Milton draws his simile,—

> " As when a Gryphon, through the wilderness,
> With winged course, o'er hill or moory dale,
> Pursues the Arimaspian, who, by stealth,
> Had from his wakeful custody purloin'd
> The guarded gold."

"O Segramour, keep the boat afloat,
  And let her na the land o'er near;
For this wicked beast will sure gae mad,
  And set fire to a' the land and mair."—

Syne has he bent an arblast bow,
  And aim'd an arrow at her head;
And swore if she didna quit the land,
  Wi' that same shaft to shoot her dead.

"O out of my stythe I winna rise,
  (And it is not for the awe o' thee,)
Till Kempion, the kingis son,
  Cum to the crag, and thrice kiss me."—

He has louted him o'er the dizzy crag,
  And gien the monster kisses ane;
Awa she gaed, and again she cam,
  The fieryest beast that ever was seen.

"O out o' my stythe I winna rise,
  (And not for a' thy bow nor thee,)
Till Kempion, the kingis son,
  Cum to the crag, and thrice kiss me."—

He's louted him o'er the Estmere crags,
  And he has gi'en her kisses twa:
Awa she gaed, and again she cam,
  The fieryest beast that ever you saw.

"O out of my den I winna rise,
　Nor flee it for the fear o' thee,
Till Kempion, that courteous knight,
　Cum to the crag, and thrice kiss me."—

He's louted him o'er the lofty crag,
　And he has gi'en her kisses three:
Awa she gaed, and again she cam,
　The loveliest ladye e'er could be!

"And by my sooth," says Kempion,
　"My ain true love, (for this is she,)
They surely had a heart o' stane,
　Could put thee to such misery.

"O was it warwolf in the wood?[1]
　Or was it mermaid in the sea?

---

[1] Warwolf, or Lycanthropus, signifies a magician, possessing the power of transforming himself into a wolf, for the purpose of ravage and devastation. It is probable the word was first used symbolically, to distinguish those, who, by means of intoxicating herbs, could work their passions into a frantic state, and throw themselves upon their enemies with the fury and temerity of ravenous wolves. Such were the noted *Berserkar* of the Scandinavians, who, in their fits of voluntary frenzy, were wont to perform the most astonishing exploits of strength, and to perpetrate the most horrible excesses, although, in their natural state, they neither were capable of greater crimes nor exertions than ordinary men. This quality they ascribed to Odin. "*Odinus efficere valuit ut hostes ipsius inter bellandum cæci vel surdi vel attoniti fierent armaque illorum instar baculorum obtusa essent. Sui vero milites sine*

Or was it man or vile woman,
 My ain true love, that mishaped thee?"—

loricis incedebant, ac instar canum vel luporum furebant scuta sua arrodentes: et robusti ut ursi vel tauri, adversarios trucidabant: ipsis vero neque ignis neque ferrum nocuit. Ea qualitas vocatur furor Berserkicus."—*Snorro Sturleson,* quoted by *Bartholin. de causis contemptæ mortis,* p. 344. For a fuller account of these frantic champions, see the *Hervarar Saga,* published by Suhm; also the *Christni Saga,* and most of the ancient Norwegian histories and romances. Camden explains the tales of the Irish, concerning men transformed into wolves, upon nearly the same principle.—*Gough's edition of Camden's Britannia,* vol. iii. p. 520.

But, in process of time, the transformation into a wolf was believed to be real, and to affect the body as well as the mind; and to such transformations our faithful Gervase of Tilbury bears evidence, as an eyewitness. " *Vidimus frequenter in Anglia per lunationes homines in lupos mutari, quod hominum genus Oerulfos Galli vocant, Angli vero* WER-WLF *dicunt.* WER *enim Anglice virum sonat,* WLF *lupum." Ot. Imp. De oculis apertis post peccatum.* The learned commentators upon the art of sorcery differ widely concerning the manner in which the arch-fiend effects this change upon the persons of his vassals; whether by surrounding their bodies with a sort of *pelisse* of condensed air, having the form of a wolf; or whether by some delusion, affecting the eyes of spectators; or, finally, by an actual corporeal transformation. The curious reader may consult *Delrii Disquisitiones Magicæ,* p. 188; and (if he pleases) Evvichius *de Natura Sagarum*—Fincelius, *lib.* 2. *de Mirac.*—Remigius *lib.* 2. *de Dæmonolat.*—Binsfield. *de Confession. Maleficarum;* not to mention Spondanus, Bodinus, Peucerus, Philippus Camerarius, Condronchus, Petrus Thyræus, Bartholomeus Spineus, Sir George Mackenzie, and King James I., with the sapient Monsieur Oufle of Bayle. The Editor presumes, it is only since the extirpation of wolves that our British sorceresses have adopted the disguise of hares, cats, and such more familiar animals.

A wild story of a war-wolf, or rather a war-bear, is told in Tor-

"It wasna warwolf in the wood,
 Nor was it mermaid in the sea;
But it was my wicked step-mother,
 And wae and weary may she be!"—

torus' History of Hrolfe Kraka. As the original is a scarce book, little known in this country, some readers may be interested by a short analysis of the tale.

Hringo, King of Upland, had an only son, called Biorno, the most beautiful and most gallant of the Norwegian youth. At an advanced period of life, the king became enamoured of a "*witch lady*," whom he chose for his second wife. A mutual and tender affection had, from infancy, subsisted betwixt Biorno and Bera, the lovely daughter of an ancient warrior. But the new queen cast upon her step-son an eye of incestuous passion; to gratify which, she prevailed upon her husband, when he set out upon one of those piratical expeditions, which formed the summer campaign of a Scandinavian monarch, to leave the prince at home. In the absence of Hringo, she communicated to Biorno her impure affection, and was repulsed with disdain and violence. The rage of the weird step-mother was boundless. "Hence to the woods!" she exclaimed, striking the prince with a glove of wolf-skin; "Hence to the woods! subsist only on thy father's herds; live pursuing, and die pursued!" From this time the Prince Biorno was no more seen, and the herdsmen of the king's cattle soon observed that astonishing devastation was nightly made among their flocks, by a black bear, of immense size and unusual ferocity. Every attempt to snare or destroy this animal was found vain; and much was the unavailing regret for the absence of Biorno, whose delight had been in extirpating beasts of prey. Bera, the faithful mistress of the young prince, added her tears to the sorrow of the people. As she was indulging her melancholy, apart from society, she was alarmed by the approach of the monstrous bear, which was the dread of the whole country. Unable to escape, she waited its approach, in expectation of instant death; when, to her astonishment, the animal fawned upon her, rolled himself at her feet, and regarded her with

" O, a heavier weird shall light her on,
    Than ever fell on vile woman;
Her hair shall grow rough, and her teeth grow lang,
    And on her four feet shall she gang."

eyes, in which, spite of the horrible transformation, she still recognised the glances of her lost lover. Bera had the courage to follow the bear to his cavern, where, during certain hours, the spell permitted him to resume his human shape. Her love overcame her repugnance at so strange a mode of life, and she continued to inhabit the cavern of Biorno, enjoying his society during the periods of his freedom from enchantment. One day, looking sadly upon his wife, "Bera," said the prince, "the end of my life approaches. My flesh will soon serve for the repast of my father and his courtiers. But do thou beware lest either the threats or entreaties of my diabolical step-mother induce thee to partake of the horrid banquet. So thou shalt safely bring forth three sons, who shall be the wonder of the North." The spell now operated, and the unfortunate prince sallied from his cavern to prowl among the herds. Bera followed him, weeping, and at a distance. The clamour of the chase was now heard. It was the old king, who, returned from his piratical excursion, had collected a strong force to destroy the devouring animal which ravaged his country. The poor bear defended himself gallantly, slaying many dogs, and some huntsmen. At length wearied out, he sought protection at the feet of his father. But his supplicating gestures were in vain, and the eyes of paternal affection proved more dull than those of love. Biorno died by the lance of his father, and his flesh was prepared for the royal banquet. Bera was recognised, and hurried into the queen's presence. The sorceress, as Biorno had predicted, endeavoured to prevail upon Bera to eat of what was then esteemed a regal dainty. Entreaties and threats being in vain, force was, by the queen's command, employed for this purpose, and Bera was compelled to swallow one morsel of the bear's flesh. A second was put into her mouth, but she had an opportunity of putting it aside. She was then dismissed to her father's house. Here, in process of time, she was delivered

"None shall take pity her upon;
  In Wormeswood she aye shall won;
And relieved shall she never be,
  Till St Mungo¹ come over the sea."—
And, sighing, said that weary wight,
  "I doubt that day I'll never see!"

of three sons, two of whom were affected variously, in person and disposition, by the share their mother had been compelled to take in the feast of the king. The eldest, from his middle downwards, resembled an elk, whence he derived the name of Elgford. He proved a man of uncommon strength, but of savage manners, and adopted the profession of a robber. Thorer, the second son of Bera, was handsome and well-shaped, saving that he had the foot of a dog, from which he obtained the appellation of Houndsfoot. But Bodvar, the third son, was a model of perfection in mind and body. He revenged upon the necromantic queen the death of his father, and became the most celebrated champion of his age.— *Historia Hrolfi Krakæ Haffniæ,* 1715. [The curious reader is referred to " The ancient English Romance of William and the Werwolf, edited from an unique copy in King's College Library, Cambridge, with an Introduction by Frederick Madden, Esq.;" printed for the Roxburghe Club in 1832.—ED.]

¹ *St Mungo*—St Kentigern.

LORD THOMAS AND FAIR ANNIE.

NOW FIRST PUBLISHED IN A PERFECT STATE.

THIS ballad is now, for the first time, published in a perfect state. A fragment, comprehending the 2d, 4th, 5th, and 6th verses, as also the 17th, has appeared in several collections. The present copy is chiefly taken from the recitation of an old woman, residing near Kirkhill, in West Lothian; the same from whom were obtained the variations in the tale of *Tamlane*, and the fragment of the *Wife of Usher's Well*, which is the next in order.

The tale is much the same with the Breton romance, called *Lay le Frain*, or the *Song of the Ash*. Indeed, the Editor is convinced, that the further our researches are extended, the more we shall see ground to believe, that the romantic ballads of later times are, for the most part, abridgements of the ancient metrical romances, narrated in a smoother stanza and more modern language. A copy of the ancient romance alluded to is preserved in the invaluable collection (W. 4. 1.) of the Advocates' Library, and begins thus:

"We redeth oft and findeth ywrite
And this clerkes wele it wite
Layes that ben in harping
Ben yfound of ferli thing
Sum beth of wer and some of wo
Sum of joye and mirthe also
And sum of trecherie and gile
Of old aventours that fel while
And sum of bourdes and ribaudy
And many ther beth of faery
Of al thinges that men seth
Maist o' love forsoth yai beth.

"In Breytene bi hold time
This layes were wrought to soithe this rime
When kinges might our y here
Of ani mervailes that ther wer
They token a harp in glee and game
And maked a lay and gaf it name
Now of this aventours that weren y falle
Y can tell sum ac nought alle
Ac herkeneth Lordinges sothe to sain
I chil you tel *Lay Le Frain*
Befel a cas in Breteyne
Whereof was made Lay Le Frain
In Ingliche for to tellen y wis
Of ane ashe forsothe it is
On ane ensamnple fair with alle
That sum tyme was bi falle," &c.

A ballad, agreeing in every respect with that which follows, exists in the Danish collection of ancient songs entitled Kæmpe Viser. It is called *Skiæn Anna*, i. e. Fair Annie; and has been translated literally by my learned friend, Mr Robert Jamieson.—See his " Po-

pular Ballads," Edin. 1806, vol. ii. p. 100. This
work contains many original and curious observations
on the connexion between the ancient poetry of Britain
and of the northern nations.

LORD THOMAS AND FAIR ANNIE.

" It's narrow, narrow, make your bed,
  And learn to lie your lane;
For I'm gaun o'er the sea, Fair Annie,
  A braw bride to bring hame.
Wi' her I will get gowd and gear;
  Wi' you I ne'er got nane.

" But wha will bake my bridal bread,
  Or brew my bridal ale?
And wha will welcome my brisk bride,
  That I bring o'er the dale?"—

" It's I will bake your bridal bread,
  And brew your bridal ale;
And I will welcome your brisk bride,
  That you bring o'er the dale."—

" But she that welcomes my brisk bride
  Maun gang like maiden fair;
She maun lace on her robe sae jimp,
  And braid her yellow hair."—

" But how can I gang maiden-like,
  When maiden I am nane?
Have I not born seven sons to thee,
  And am with child again?"—

She's ta'en her young son in her arms,
  Another in her hand;
And she's up to the highest tower,
  To see him come to land.

" Come up, come up, my eldest son,
  And look o'er yon sea-strand,
And see your father's new-come bride
  Before she come to land."—

" Come down, come down, my mother dear,
  Come frae the castle-wa'!
I fear, if langer ye stand there,
  Ye'll let yoursell down fa'."—

And she gaed down, and farther down,
  Her love's ship for to see;
And the topmast and the mainmast
  Shone like the silver free.

And she's gane down, and farther down,
  The bride's ship to behold;
And the topmast and the mainmast
  They shone just like the gold.

She's ta'en her seven sons in her hand;
    I wot she didna fail!
She met Lord Thomas and his bride,
    As they came o'er the dale.

" You're welcome to your house, Lord Thomas;
    You're welcome to your land;
You're welcome, with your fair ladye,
    That you lead by the hand.

" You're welcome to your ha's, ladye,
    Your welcome to your bowers;
You're welcome to your hame, ladye,
    For a' that's here is yours."—

" I thank thee, Annie; I thank thee, Annie;
    Sae dearly as I thank thee;
You're the likest to my sister Annie,
    That ever I did see.

" There came a knight out o'er the sea,
    And steal'd my sister away;
The shame scoup[1] in his company,
    And land where'er he gae!"—

She hang ae napkin at the door,
    Another in the ha';

---

[1] *Scoup*—Go, or rather fly.

And a' to wipe the trickling tears,
　　Sae fast as they did fa'.

And aye she served the lang tables
　　With white bread and with wine;
And aye she drank the wan water,
　　To had her colour fine.[1]

And aye she served the lang tables,
　　With white bread and with brown;
And ay she turn'd her round about,
　　Sae fast the tears fell down.

And he's ta'en down the silk napkin,
　　Hung on a silver pin;
And aye he wipes the tear trickling
　　Adown her cheek and chin.

And aye he turn'd him round about,
　　And smiled amang his men,
Says—" Like ye best the old ladye,
　　Or her that's new come hame?"—

When bells were rung, and mass was sung,
　　And a' men bound to bed,
Lord Thomas and his new-come bride,
　　To their chamber they were gaed.

[1] To keep her from changing countenance.

Annie made her bed a little forbye,
    To hear what they might say;
" And ever alas!" fair Annie cried,
    " That I should see this day!

" Gin my seven sons were seven young rats,
    Running on the castle-wa',
And I were a grey cat mysell,
    I soon would worry them a'.

" Gin my seven sons were seven young hares,
    Running o'er yon lilly lee,
And I were a grew hound mysell,
    Soon worried they a' should be."—

And wae and sad fair Annie sat,
    And drearie was her sang;
And ever, as she sobb'd and grat,
    " Wae to the man that did the wrang!"—

" My gown is on," said the new-come bride,
    " My shoes are on my feet,
And I will to fair Annie's chamber,
    And see what gars her greet.——

" What ails ye, what ails ye, Fair Annie,
    That ye make sic a moan?
Has your wine barrels cast the girds,
    Or is your white bread gone?

" O wha was't was your father, Annie,
 Or wha was't was your mother?
And had you ony sister, Annie,
 Or had you ony brother?"—

" The Earl of Wemyss was my father,
 The Countess of Wemyss my mother:
And a' the folk about the house,
 To me were sister and brother."—

" If the Earl of Wemyss was your father,
 I wot sae was he mine;
And it shall not be for lack o' gowd,
 That ye your love sall tyne.—

" For I have seven ships o' mine ain,
 A' loaded to the brim;
And I will gie them a' to thee,
 Wi' four to thine eldest son.
But thanks to a' the powers in heaven,
 That I gae maiden hume!"—

THE WIFE OF USHER'S WELL.

A FRAGMENT.

NEVER BEFORE PUBLISHED.

There lived a wife at Usher's Well,
    And a wealthy wife was she,
She had three stout and stalwart sons,
    And sent them o'er the sea.

They hadna been a week from her,
    A week but barely ane,
When word came to the carline wife,
    That her three sons were gane.

They hadna been a week from her,
    A week but barely three,
When word came to the carline wife,
    That her sons she'd never see.

THE WIFE OF USHER'S WELL, CONTINUED.

stalwart sons, And she sent them o'er the sea.

" I wish the wind may never cease,[1]
  Nor fishes[2] in the flood,
Till my three sons come hame to me,
  In earthly flesh and blood!"—

It fell about the Martinmas,
  When nights are lang and mirk,
The carline wife's three sons came hame.
  And their hats were o' the birk.

It neither grew in syke nor ditch,
  Nor yet in ony sheugh;
But at the gates o' Paradise,
  That birk grew fair eneugh.[3]

* * * * * * *

[1] The sense of this verse is obscure, owing, probably, to corruption by reciters. It would appear that the mother had sinned in the same degree with the celebrated *Lenoré*.

[2] [Query. Should we not read, for *fishes* here, *fashes*—i. e. troubles?—ED.]

[3] The notion, that the souls of the blessed wear garlands, seems to be of Jewish origin. At least in the *Muase-book*, there is a Rabbinical tradition to the following effect:—

" It fell out, that a Jew, whose name was Ponim, an ancient man, whose business was altogether about the dead, coming to the door of the school, saw one standing there, who had a garland upon his head. Then was Rabbi Ponim afraid, imagining it was a spirit. Whereupon he, whom the Rabbi saw, called out to him, saying, ' Be not afraid, but pass forward. Dost thou not know me?"

"Blow up the fire, my maidens!
Bring water from the well!
For a' my house shall feast this night,
Since my three sons are well."—

And she has made to them a bed,
She's made it large and wide;

Then said Rabbi Ponim, 'Art thou not he whom I buried yesterday?' And he was answered, 'Yes, I am he.' Upon which Rabbi Ponim said, 'Why comest thou hither? How fareth it with thee in the other world?' And the apparition made answer, 'It goeth well with me, and I am in high esteem in Paradise.' Then said the Rabbi, 'Thou wert but looked upon in the world as an insignificant Jew. What good work didst thou do, that thou art thus esteemed?' The apparition answered, 'I will tell thee: the reason of the esteem I am in, is, that I rose every morning early, and with fervency uttered my prayer, and offered the grace from the bottom of my heart; for which reason I now pronounce grace in Paradise, and am well respected. If thou doubtest whether I am the person, I will shew thee a token that will convince thee of it. Yesterday, when thou didst clothe me in my funeral attire, thou didst tear my sleeve.' Then asked Rabbi Ponim, 'What is the meaning of that garland?' The apparition answered, 'I wear it, to the end the wind of the world may not have power over me; for it consists of excellent herbs of Paradise.' Then did Rabbi Ponim mend the sleeve of the deceased; for the deceased had said, that if it was not mended, he should be ashamed to be seen amongst others, whose apparel was whole. And then the apparition vanished. Wherefore, let every one utter his prayer with fervency; for then it shall go well with him in the other world. And let care be taken that no rent, nor tearing, be left in the apparel in which the deceased are interred."—*Jewish Traditions, abridged from Buxtorf*, London, 1732, vol. ii. p. 19.

And she's ta'en her mantle her about,
  Sat down at the bed-side.

*   *   *   *   *   *   *

Up then crew the red red cock,
  And up and crew the gray;
The eldest to the youngest said,
  " 'Tis time we were away."—

The cock he hadna craw'd but once,
  And clapp'd his wings at a',
When the youngest to the eldest said,
  " Brother, we must awa.—

" The cock doth craw, the day doth daw,
  The channerin'[1] worm doth chide;
Gin we be mist out o' our place,
  A sair pain we maun bide.[2]

---

[1] *Channerin'*—Fretting.

[2] This will remind the German reader of the comic adieu of a heavenly apparition:—

> " Doch sieh! man schliesst die himmels thür;
> Adieu! der himmlische Portier
> Ist streng und hält auf ordnung."
>
>   *Blumauer.*

"Fare ye weel, my mother dear!
Fareweel to barn and byre!
And fare ye weel, the bonny lass,
That kindles my mother's fire."

* * * * * * *

COSPATRICK.

NEVER BEFORE PUBLISHED.

A copy of this Ballad, materially different from that which follows, appeared in " Scottish Songs," *2 vols. Edinburgh, 1792, under the title of* Lord Bothwell. *Some stanzas have been transferred from thence to the present copy, which is taken down from the recitation of a Lady, nearly related to the Editor.*[1] *Some readings have been also adopted from a third copy, in Mrs* BROWN'S MS., *under the title of* Child Brenton. *Cospatrick* (Comes Patricius) *was the designation of the Earl of Dunbar, in the days of* WALLACE *and* BRUCE.

COSPATRICK has sent o'er the faem;
Cospatrick brought his ladye hame;
And fourscore ships have come her wi',
The ladye by the grene-wood tree.

There were twal' and twal' wi' baken bread,
And twal' and twal' wi' gowd sae reid,
And twal' and twal' wi' bouted flour,
And twal' and twal' wi' the paramour.

---
[1] [Miss Christian Rutherford, sister to Sir Walter Scott's mother.—ED.]

Sweet Willy was a widow's son,
And at her stirrup he did run;
And she was clad in the finest pall,
But aye she let the tears down fall.

" O is your saddle set awrye?
Or rides your steed for you ower high?
Or are you mourning, in your tide,
That you suld be Cospatrick's bride?"—

" I am not mourning, at this tide,
That I suld be Cospatrick's bride;
But I am sorrowing in my mood,
That I suld leave my mother good.

" But, gentle boy, come tell 'to me,
What is the custom of thy countrie?"—
" The custom thereof, my dame," he says,
" Will ill a gentle ladye please.

" Seven king's daughters has our lord wedded,
And seven king's daughters has our lord bedded;
But he's cutted their breasts frae their breast-bane,
And sent them mourning hame again.

" Yet, gin you're sure that you're a maid,
Ye may gae safely to his bed;
But gif o' that ye be na sure,
Then hire some damsell o' your bour."—

The ladye's call'd her bour maiden,
That waiting was into her train ;
" Five thousand merks I'll gie to thee,
To sleep this night with my lord for me."—

When bells were rung, and mass was sayne,
And a' men unto bed were gane,
Cospatrick and the bonny maid,
Into a chamber they were laid.

" Now, speak to me, blankets, and speak to me, bed,
And speak, thou sheet, enchanted web ;
And speak up, my bonny brown sword, that winna lie,
Is this a true maiden that lies by me ?"—

" It is not a maid that you hae wedded,
But it is a maid that you hae bedded ;
It is a leal maiden that lies by thee,
But not the maiden that it should be."—

O wrathfully he left the bed,
And wrathfully his claes on did ;
And he has ta'en him through the ha',
And on his mother he did ca'.

" I am the most unhappy man,
That ever was in Christen land !
I courted a maiden, meik and mild,
And I hae gotten naething but a woman wi' child."—

"O stay, my son, into this ha',
And sport ye wi' your merrymen a';
And I will to the secret bour,
To see how it fares wi' your paramour."—

The carline she was stark and sture,
She aff the hinges dang the dure;
"O is your bairn to laird or loun,
Or is it to your father's groom?"—

"O hear me, mother, on my knee,
Till my sad story I tell to thee:
O we were sisters, sisters seven,
We were the fairest under heaven.

"It fell on a summer's afternoon,
When a' our toilsome task was done,
We cast the kevils us amang,
To see which suld to the grene-wood gang.

"O hon! alas, for I was youngest,
And aye my wierd it was the hardest!
The kevil it on me did fa',
Whilk was the cause of a' my woe.

"For to the grene-wood I maun gae,
To pu' the red rose and the slae;
To pu' the red rose and the thyme,
To deck my mother's bour and mine.

" I hadna pu'd a flower but ane,
When by there came a gallant bende,
Wi' high-coll'd hose and laigh-coll'd shoon,
And he seem'd to be sum kingis son.

" And be I a maid, or be I nae,
He kept me there till the close o' day ;
And be I a maid, or be I nane,
He kept me there till the day was done.

" He gae me a lock o' his yellow hair,
And bade me keep it ever mair ;
He gae me a carknet [1] o' bonny beads,
And bade me keep it against my needs.

" He gae to me a gay gold ring,
And bade me keep it abune a' thing."—
" What did ye wi' the tokens rare,
That ye gat frae that gallant there ?"—

" O bring that coffer unto me,
And a' the tokens ye sall see."—
" Now stay, daughter, your bour within,
While I gae parley wi' my son."—

---

[1] *Carknet*—A necklace. Thus :—
    " She threw away her rings and *carknet* cleen."
  HARRISON's *Translation of Orlando Furioso*—Notes on Book 37th.

O she has ta'en her thro' the ha',
And on her son began to ca';
"What did ye wi' the bonny beads
I bade you keep against your needs?

"What did you wi' the gay gold ring
I bade you keep abune a' thing?"—
"I gae them to a ladye gay,
I met on grene-wood on a day.

"But I wad gie a' my halls and tours,
I had that ladye within my bours;
But I wad gie my very life,
I had that ladye to my wife."—

"Now keep, my son, your ha's and tours,
Ye have the bright burd in your bours;
And keep, my son, your very life,
Ye have that ladye to your wife."—

Now, or a month was come and gane,
The ladye bare a bonny son;
And 'twas weel written on his breast-bane,
"Cospatrick is my father's name."
O row my lady in satin and silk,
And wash my son in the morning milk.

PRINCE ROBERT.

NEVER BEFORE PUBLISHED.

FROM THE RECITATION OF A LADY, NEARLY RELATED TO THE EDITOR.[1]

Prince Robert has wedded a gay ladye,
   He has wedded her with a ring :
Prince Robert has wedded a gay ladye,
   But he darna bring her hame.

" Your blessing, your blessing, my mother dear!
   Your blessing now grant to me !"—
" Instead of a blessing ye sall have my curse,
   And you'll get nae blessing frae me."—

She has call'd upon her waiting-maid,
   To fill a glass of wine ;
She has call'd upon her fause steward,
   To put rank poison in.

---

[1] [Miss Christian Rutherford. See p. 263, *ante*.—ED.]

She has put it to her roudes[1] lip,
    And to her roudes chin;
She has put it to her fause fause mouth,
    But the never a drap gaed in.

He has put it to his bonny mouth,
    And to his bonny chin,
He's put it to his cherry lip,
    And sae fast the rank poison ran in.

" O ye hae poison'd your ae son, mother,
    Your ae son and your heir;
O ye hae poison'd your ae son, mother,
    And sons you'll never hae mair.

" O where will I get a little boy,
    That will win hose and shoon,
To rin sae fast to Darlinton,
    And bid fair Eleanor come?"—

Then up and spake a little boy,
    That wad win hose and shoon,—
" O I'll away to Darlinton,
    And bid fair Eleanor come."—

O he has run to Darlinton,
    And tirled at the pin;
And wha was sae ready as Eleanor's sell
    To let the bonny boy in.

[1] *Roudes*—Haggard.

"Your gude-mother has made ye a rare dinour,
    She's made it baith gude and fine;
Your gude-mother has made ye a gay dinour,
    And ye maun cum till her and dine."—

It's twenty lang miles to Sillertoun town,
    The langest that ever were gane:
But the steed it was wight, and the ladye was light,
    And she cam linkin'¹ in.

But when she came to Sillertoun town,
    And into Sillertoun ha',
The torches were burning, the ladies were mourning,
    And they were weeping a'.

"O where is now my wedded lord,
    And where now can he be?
O where is now my wedded lord?
    For him I canna see."—

"Your wedded lord is dead," she says,
    "And just gane to be laid in the clay:
Your wedded lord is dead," she says,
    "And just gane to be buried the day.

"Ye'se get nane o' his gowd, ye'se get nane o' his gear,
    Ye'se get nae thing frae me;

---

¹ *Linkin'*—Riding briskly.

Ye'se no get an inch o' his gude braid land,
    Though your heart suld burst in three."—

" I want nane o' his gowd, I want nane o' his gear,
    I want nae land frae thee:
But I'll hae the rings that's on his finger,
    For them he did promise to me."—

" Ye'se no get the rings that's on his finger,
    Ye'se no get them frae me;
Ye'se no get the rings that's on his finger,
    An your heart suld burst in three."—

She's turn'd her back unto the wa',
    And her face unto a rock;
And there, before the mother's face,
    Her very heart it broke.

The tane was buried in Marie's kirk,
    The tother in Marie's quair;
And out o' the tane there sprang a birk,
    And out o' the tother a brier.

And thae twa met, and thae twa plat,
    The birk but and the brier;
And by that ye may very weel ken
    They were twa lovers dear.[1]

---

[1] The two last verses are common to many ballads, and are pro-

bably derived from some old metrical romance, since we find the idea occur in the voluminous history of Sir Tristrem. "*Ores veitil que de la tombe Tristan yssoit une belle ronce verte et feuilleuse, qui alloit par la chapelle, et descendoit le bout de la ronce sur la tumbe d'Ysseult, et entroit dedans.*" This marvellous plant was three times cut down, but, continues Rusticien de Puise, "*Le lendemain estoit aussi belle comme elle avoit cy-devant été, et ce miracle étoit sur Tristran et sur Ysseult a tout jamais advenir.*"

KING HENRIE.

THE ANCIENT COPY.

This ballad is edited from the MS. of Mrs Brown, corrected by a recited fragment. A modernized copy has been published, under the title of "Courteous King Jamie."—*Tales of Wonder*, vol. ii. p. 451.

The legend will remind the reader of the "Marriage of Sir Gawain," in the *Reliques of Ancient Poetry*, and of "The Wife of Bath's Tale," in Father Chaucer. But the original, as appears from the following quotation from Torfœus, is to be found in an Icelandic Saga.

"*Hellgius, Rex Daniæ, mœrore ob omissam conjugem vexatus, solus agebat, et subducens se hominum commercio, segregem domum, omnis famulitii impatiens, incolebat. Accidit autem, ut, nocte concubia, lamentabilis cujusdam ante fores ejulantis sonus auribus ejus obreperet. Expergefactus igitur, recluso ostio, informe quoddam mulieris simulacrum habitu corporis fœdum, veste squalore obsita, pallore, macie, rigorisque tyrannide propemodum peremptum, de-*

prehendit; quod precibus obsecratus, ut qui jam miserorum ærumnas ex propria calamitate pensare didicisset, in domum intromisit; ipse lectum petit. At mulier, ne hac quidem benignitate contenta, thori consortium obnixè flagitabat, addens id tanti referre, ut, nisi impetraret, omnino sibi moriendum esset. Quod ea lege, ne ipsum attingeret, concessum est. Ideo nec complexu eam dignatus rex avertit sese. Cum autem prima luce forte oculos ultro citroque converteret, eximiæ formæ virginem lecto receptam animadvertit; quæ statim ipsi placere cœpit: causam igitur tam repentinæ mutationis curiosius indaganti, respondit virgo, se unam e subterraneorum hominum genere diris novercalibus devotam, tam tetra et execrabili specie, quali primo comparuit, damnatam, quoad thori cujusdam principis socia fieret; multos reges hac de re sollicitasse. Jam, actis pro præstitio beneficio gratiis, discessum maturans, a rege formæ ejus illecebris capto comprimitur. Deinde petit, si prolem ex hoc congressu progigni contigerit, sequente hyeme, eodem anni tempore, ante fores positam in ædes reciperit, seque ejus patrem profiteri non gravaretur, secus non leve infortunium insecuturum prædixit: e quo præcepto cum rex postea exorbitasset, nec præ foribus jacentem infantem pro suo agnoscere voluisset, ad eum iterum, sed corrugata fronte, accessit, obque violatam fidem acrius objurgatum ab imminente periculo, præstiti olim beneficii gratia, exempturam pollicebatur, ita tamen ut, tota ultionis rabies in filium

ejus effusa, graves aliquando levitatis illius pœnas exigeret. Ex hac tam dissimilium naturarum commixtione, Skulda, versuti et versatilis animi mulier, nata fuisse memoratur; quæ utramque naturam participans prodigiosorum operum effectrix perhibetur."
— Hrolffi Krakii Hist. p. 49. Hafn. 1715.

KING HENRIE.

ANCIENT COPY.

Let never man a-wooing wend,
    That lacketh thingis thrie;
A rowth o' gold, an open heart,
    And fu' o' courtesy.

And this was seen o' King Henrie,
    For he lay burd alane;
And he has ta'en him to a haunted hunt's ha',
    Was seven miles frae a toun.

He's chased the dun deer thro' the wood,
    And the roe doun by the den,
Till the fattest buck in a' the herd
    King Henrie he has slain.

He's ta'en him to his huntin' ha',
    For to make burly cheir;
When loud the wind was heard to sound,
    And an earthquake rock'd the floor.

And darkness cover'd a' the hall,
    Where they sat at their meat;
The grey dogs, youling, left their food,
    And crept to Henrie's feet.

And louder houl'd the rising wind,
    And burst the fast'ned door;
And in there came a griesly ghost,
    Stood stamping on the floor.

Her head touch'd the roof-tree of the house;
    Her middle ye weel mot span:
Each frighted huntsman fled the ha',
    And left the King alane.

Her teeth were a' like tether-stakes,
    Her nose like club or mell:
And I ken naething she appear'd to be,
    But the fiend that wons in hell.

" Sum meat, sum meat, ye King Henrie,
    Sum meat ye gie to me!"—
" And what meat's i' this house, ladye,
    That ye're na wellcum tee?"—[1]
" O ye'se gae kill your berry-brown steed,
    And serve him up to me."

O when he kill'd his berry-brown steed,
    Wow gin his heart was sair!

---

[1] *Tee* for *to*, is the Duchanshire and Gallovidian pronunciation.

She ate him a' up, skin and bane,
    Left naething but hide and hair.

"Mair meat, mair meat, ye King Henrie!
    Mair meat ye gie to me!"—
"And what meat's i' this house, ladye,
    That ye're na wellcum tee?"—
"O ye do slay your gude grey houndes,
    And bring them a' to me."—

O when he slew his gude grey houndes,
    Wow but his heart was sair!
She's ate them a' up, ane by ane,
    Left naething but hide and hair.

"Mair meat, mair meat, ye King Henrie!
    Mair meat ye gie to me!"—
"And what meat's i' this house, ladye,
    That I hae left to gie?"—
"O ye do fell your gay goss-hawks,
    And bring them a' to me."—

O when he fell'd his gay goss-hawks,
    Wow but his heart was sair!
She's ate them a' up, bane by bane,
    Left naething but feathers bare.

"Some drink, some drink, ye King Henrie!
    Some drink ye gie to me!"—

" And what drink's i' this house, ladye,
    That ye're na wellcum tee?"—
" O ye sew up your horse's hide,
    And bring in a drink to me."—

O he has sew'd up the bluidy hide,
    And put in a pipe of wine;
She drank it a' up at ae draught,
    Left na a drap therein.

" A bed, a bed, ye King Henrie!
    A bed ye mak to me!"—
" And what's the bed i' this house, ladye,
    That ye're na wellcum tee?"—
" O ye maun pu' the green heather,
    And mak a bed to me."—

O pu'd has he the heather green,
    And made to her a bed;
And up he has ta'en his gay mantle,
    And o'er it he has spread.

" Now swear, now swear, ye King Henrie,
    To take me for your bride!"—
" O God forbid," King Henrie said,
    " That e'er the like betide!
That e'er the fiend that wons in hell
    Should streak down by my side."—

* * * * * * *

When day was come, and night was gane,
  And the sun shone through the ha',
The fairest ladye that e'er was seen,
  Lay atween him and the wa'.

" O weel is me!" King Henrie said,
  " How lang will this last wi' me?"—
And out and spak that ladye fair,
  " E'en till the day ye die.

" For I was witch'd to a ghastly shape,
  All by my stepdame's skill,
Till I should meet wi' a courteous knight,
  Wad gie me a' my will."

ANNAN WATER.

NEVER BEFORE PUBLISHED.

The following verses are the original words of the tune of "*Allan Water*," by which name the song is mentioned in Ramsay's *Tea Table Miscellany*. The ballad is given from tradition; and it is said that a bridge, over the Annan, was built in consequence of the melancholy catastrophe which it narrates. Two verses are added in this edition, from another copy of the ballad, in which the conclusion proves fortunate. By the *Gatehope-Slack*, is perhaps meant the *Gate-Slack*, a pass in Annandale. The Annan, and the Frith of Solway, into which it falls, are the frequent scenes of tragical accidents. The Editor trusts he will be pardoned for inserting the following awfully impressive account of such an event, contained in a letter from Dr Currie, of Liverpool, by whose correspondence, while in the course of preparing these volumes for the press, he has been alike honoured and instructed. After stating that he had some recollection of the ballad which follows, the biographer of Burns proceeds thus:—" I once in my early days heard (for it was night, and I could not see) a traveller drowning; not in the Annan itself, but in the Frith of Solway, close by the mouth of that river. The influx of the tide had unhorsed him, in the night, as he was passing the sands from Cumberland. The west wind blew a tempest, and, according to the common expression, brought in the water *three foot a-breast*. The traveller got upon a standing net, a little way from the shore. There he lashed himself to the post, shouting for half an hour for assistance—till the tide rose over his head! In the darkness of the night, and amid the pauses of the hurricane, his voice, heard at intervals, was exquisitely mournful. No one could go to his assistance—no one knew where he was—the sound seemed to proceed from the spirit of the waters. But morning rose—the tide had ebbed—and the poor traveller was found lashed to the pole of the net, and bleaching in the wind."

ANNAN WATER.

"Annan water's wading deep,
   And my love Annie's wondrous bonny;
And I am laith she suld weet her feet,
   Because I love her best of ony.

"Gar saddle me the bonny black,
   Gar saddle sune, and make him ready;
For I will down the Gatehope-Slack,
   And all to see my bonny ladye."—

He has loupen on the bonny black,
   He stirr'd him wi' the spur right sairly;
But, or he wan the Gatehope-Slack,
   I think the steed was wae and weary.

He has loupen on the bonny grey,
   He rade the right gate and the ready;
I trow he would neither stint nor stay,
   For he was seeking his bonny ladye.

O he has ridden o'er field and fell,
   Through muir and moss, and mony a mire:

His spurs o' steel were sair to bide,
    And frae her fore-feet flew the fire.

" Now, bonny grey, now play your part!
    Gin ye be the steed that wins my deary,
Wi' corn and hay ye'se be fed for aye,
    And never spur sall make you wearie."—

The grey was a mare, and a right good mare;
    But when she wan the Annan water,
She couldna hae ridden a furlong mair,
    Had a thousand merks been wadded[1] at her.

" O boatman, boatman, put off your boat!
    Put off your boat for gowden money!
I cross the drumly stream the night,
    Or never mair I see my honey."—

" O I was sworn sae late yestreen,
    And not by ae aith, but by many;
And for a' the gowd in fair Scotland,
    I dare na take ye through to Annie."—

The side was stey, and the bottom deep,
    Frae bank to brae the water pouring;
And the bonny grey mare did sweat for fear,
    For she heard the water kelpy roaring.

[1] *Wadded*—Wagered.

O he has pou'd aff his dapperpy[1] coat,
   The silver buttons glanced bonny;
The waistcoat bursted aff his breast,
   He was sae full of melancholy.

He has ta'en the ford at that stream tail;
   I wot he swam both strong and steady,
But the stream was broad, and his strength did fail,
   And he never saw his bonny ladye!

" O wae betide the frush[2] saugh wand!
   And wae betide the bush of brier,
It brake into my true love's hand,
   When his strength did fail, and his limbs did tire.

" And wae betide ye, Annan Water,
   This night that ye are a drumlie river!
For over thee I'll build a bridge,
   That ye never more true love may sever."—

---

[1] *Query*—Cap-a-pee?—[2] *Frush*—Brittle; without cohesion of parts.

THE CRUEL SISTER.

This ballad differs essentially from that which has been published in various collections, under the title of *Binnorie*. It is compiled from a copy in Mrs Brown's MSS., intermixed with a beautiful fragment, of fourteen verses, transmitted to the Editor by J. C. Walker, Esq. the ingenious historian of the Irish bards. Mr Walker, at the same time, favoured the Editor with the following note:—" I am indebted to my departed friend, Miss Brook, for the foregoing pathetic fragment. Her account of it was as follows:—This song was transcribed, several years ago, from the memory of an old woman, who had no recollection of the concluding verses: probably the beginning may also be lost, as it seems to commence abruptly." The first verse and burden of the fragment ran thus:—

> "O sister, sister, reach thy hand!
> Hey ho, my Nanny, O;
> And you shall be heir of all my land,
> While the swan swims bonny, O."

The first part of this chorus seems to be corrupted

from the common burden of *Hey Nonny, Nonny*, alluded to in the song, beginning, "*Sigh no more, ladyes.*" The chorus, retained in this edition, is the most common and popular; but Mrs Brown's copy[1] bears a yet different burden, beginning thus;—

> "There were twa sisters sat in a bour,
>   Edinborough, Edinborough;
> There were twa sisters sat in a bour,
>   Stirling for aye;
> There were twa sisters sat in a bour,
> There cam a knight to be their wooer,
>   Bonny St Johnston stands upon Tay."

The ballad, being probably very popular, was the subject of a parody, which is to be found in D'Urfey's "Pills to purge Melancholy."

[1] [Mr Jamieson has printed Mrs Brown's copy *verbatim*, under the title of "The Twa Sisters."—*Popular Ballads*, 1806, vol. i. p. 50.—Ed.]

THE CRUEL SISTER.

There were two sisters sat in a bour;
>   Binnorie, O Binnorie;[1]
There came a knight to be their wooer;
>   By the bonny milldams of Binnorie.

He courted the eldest with glove and ring,
>   Binnorie, O Binnorie;
But he lo'ed the youngest abune a' thing;
>   By the bonny milldams of Binnorie.

He courted the eldest with broach and knife,
>   Binnorie, O Binnorie;
But he lo'ed the youngest abune his life;
>   By the bonny milldams of Binnorie.

The eldest she was vexed sair,
>   Binnorie, O Binnorie;
And sore envied her sister fair;
>   By the bonny milldams of Binnorie.

[1] [Pronounced Binnŏrie.—Ed.]

The eldest said to the youngest ane,
   Binnorie, O Binnorie;
" Will ye go and see our father's ships come in ?"—
   By the bonny milldams of Binnorie.

She's ta'en her by the lily hand,
   Binnorie, O Binnorie;
And led her down to the river strand;
   By the bonny milldams of Binnorie.

The youngest stude upon a stane,
   Binnorie, O Binnorie;
The eldest came and pushed her in;
   By the bonny milldams of Binnorie.

She took her by the middle sma',
   Binnorie, O Binnorie;
And dash'd her bonny back to the jaw;
   By the bonny milldams of Binnorie.

" O sister, sister, reach your hand,
   Binnorie, O Binnorie;
And ye shall be heir of half my land."—
   By the bonny milldams of Binnorie.

" O sister, I'll not reach my hand,
   Binnorie, O Binnorie;
And I'll be heir of all your land;
   By the bonny milldams of Binnorie.

" Shame fa' the hand that I should take,
   Binnorie, O Binnorie;
It's twin'd me, and my world's make."—
   By the bonny milldams of Binnorie.

" O sister, reach me but your glove,
   Binnorie, O Binnorie;
And sweet William shall be your love."—
   By the bonny milldams of Binnorie.

" Sink on, nor hope for hand or glove!
   Binnorie, O Binnorie:
And sweet William shall better be my love,
   By the bonny milldams of Binnorie.

" Your cherry cheeks and your yellow hair,
   Binnorie, O Binnorie;
Garr'd me gang maiden evermair."—
   By the bonny milldams of Binnorie.

Sometimes she sunk, and sometimes she swam,
   Binnorie, O Binnorie;
Until she cam to the miller's dam;
   By the bonny milldams of Binnorie.

" O father, father, draw your dam!
   Binnorie, O Binnorie;
There's either a mermaid, or a milk-white swan."—
   By the bonny milldams of Binnorie.

The miller hasted and drew his dam,
   Binnorie, O Binnorie;
And there he found a drown'd woman;
   By the bonny milldams of Binnorie.

You could not see her yellow hair,
   Binnorie, O Binnorie;
For gowd and pearls that were so rare;
   By the bonny milldams of Binnorie.

You could not see her middle sma',
   Binnorie, O Binnorie;
Her gowden girdle was sae bra';
   By the bonny milldams of Binnorie.

A famous harper passing by,
   Binnorie, O Binnorie:
The sweet pale face he chanced to spy;
   By the bonny milldams of Binnorie.

And when he looked that lady on,
   Binnorie, O Binnorie;
He sigh'd and made a heavy moan;
   By the bonny milldams of Binnorie.

He made a harp of her breast-bone,
   Binnorie, O Binnorie;
Whose sounds would melt a heart of stone;
   By the bonny milldams of Binnorie.

The strings he framed of her yellow hair,
              Binnorie, O Binnorie;
Whose notes made sad the listening ear;
              By the bonny milldams of Binnorie.

He brought it to her father's hall,
              Binnorie, O Binnorie;
And there was the court assembled all;
              By the bonny milldams of Binnorie.

He laid his harp upon a stone,
              Binnorie, O Binnorie;
And straight it began to play alone;
              By the bonny milldams of Binnorie.

" O yonder sits my father, the king,
              Binnorie, O Binnorie;
And yonder sits my mother, the queen;
              By the bonny milldams of Binnorie.

" And yonder stands my brother Hugh,
              Binnorie, O Binnorie;
And by him my William, sweet and true."—
              By the bonny milldams of Binnorie.

But the last tune that the harp play'd then,
              Binnorie, O Binnorie;
Was—" Woe to my sister, false Helen!"—
              By the bonny milldams of Binnorie.

THE QUEEN'S MARIE.

NEVER BEFORE PUBLISHED.

"In the very time of the General Assembly, there comes to public knowledge a haynous murther, committed in the court; yea, not far from the Queen's lap; for a French woman, that served in the Queen's chamber, had played the whore with the Queen's own apothecary.—The woman conceived and bare a childe, whom, with common consent, the father and mother murthered; yet were the cries of a new-borne childe hearde, searche was made, the childe and the mother were both apprehended, and so were the man and the woman condemned to be hanged in the publicke street of Edinburgh. The punishment was suitable, because the crime was haynous. But yet was not the court purged of whores and whoredoms, which was the fountaine of such enormities; for it was well known that shame hasted marriage betwixt John Sempill, called the Dancer, and Mary Levingston,[1] sirnamed the Lusty.

[1] "John Semple, son of Robert, Lord Semple, (by Elizabeth

What bruit the Maries, and the rest of the dancers of the court had, *the ballads of that age* doe witnesse, which we for modestie's sake omit: but this was the common complaint of all godly and wise men, that if they thought such a court could long continue, and if they looked for no better life to come, they would have wished their sonnes and daughters rather to have been brought up with fiddlers and dancers, and to have been exercised with flinging upon a floore, and in the rest that thereof followes, than to have been exercised in the company of the godly, and exercised in virtue, which in that court was hated, and filthenesse not only maintained, but also rewarded: witnesse the Abbey of Abercorne, the Barony of Auchtermuchtie, and divers others, pertaining to the patrimony of the crown, given in heritage to skippers and dancers, and dalliers with dames. This was the beginning of the regiment of Mary, Queen of Scots, and these were the fruits that she brought forth of France.—*Lord! look on our miseries! and deliver us from the wickedness of this corrupt court!*"—KNOX's *History of the Reformation*, p. 373-4.

Such seems to be the subject of the following ballad,

Carlisle, a daughter of the Lord Torthorald,) was ancestor of the Semples of Beltrees. He was married to Mary, sister to William Livingston, and one of the maids of honour to Queen Mary; by whom he had Sir James Semple of Beltrees, his son and heir," &c.; afterwards ambassador to England, for King James VI., in 1599.—CRAWFORD's *History of Renfrew*, p. 101.

as narrated by the stern apostle of Presbytery. It will readily strike the reader, that the tale has suffered great alterations, as handed down by tradition; the French waiting-woman being changed into Mary Hamilton,[1] and the Queen's apothecary into Henry Darnley. Yet this is less surprising, when we recollect, that one of the heaviest of the Queen's complaints against her ill-

---

[1] One copy bears, "*Mary Miles.*" A very odd coincidence in name, crime, and catastrophe, occurred at the Court of Czar Peter the Great. It is thus detailed by the obliging correspondent who recommended it to my notice:—

"Miss Hambleton, a maid of honour to the Empress Catherine, had an amour, which, at different times, produced three children. She had always pleaded sickness, but Peter, being suspicious, ordered his physician to attend her, who soon made the discovery. It also appeared, that a sense of shame had triumphed over her humanity, and that the children had been put to death as soon as born. Peter enquired if the father of them was privy to the murder; the lady insisted that he was innocent; for she had always deceived him, by pretending that they were sent to nurse. Justice now called upon the Emperor to punish the offence. The lady was much beloved by the Empress, who pleaded for her; the amour was pardonable, but not the murder. Peter sent her to the castle, and went himself to visit her; and the fact being confessed, he pronounced her sentence with tears; telling her, that his duty as a prince, and God's vicegerent, called on him for that justice which her crime had rendered indispensably necessary; and that she must therefore prepare for death. He attended her also on the scaffold, where he embraced her with the utmost tenderness, mixed with sorrow; and some say, when the head was struck off, he took it up by the ear, whilst the lips were still trembling, and kissed them; a circumstance of an extraordinary nature, and yet not incredible, considering the peculiarities of his character."

fated husband, was his infidelity, and that even with her personal attendants. I have been enabled to publish the following complete edition of the ballad, by copies from various quarters; that principally used was communicated to me, in the most polite manner, by Mr Kirkpatricke Sharpe, of Hoddom, to whom I am indebted for many similar favours.[1]

[1] [Mr Kinloch has printed a north country version of this ballad, differing considerably from that in the text. See his *Ballads*, 1827, p. 252. He also gives a *fragment* of a third version, viz.—

"My father is the Duke of Argyle,
My mother's a lady gay;
And I, myself, am a dainty dame,
And the King desired me.

"He shaw'd me up, he shaw'd me down,
He shaw'd me to the ha';
He shaw'd me to the low cellars,
And that was warst of a'."

Mr Motherwell has also given a west country version of this ballad, under the title of "Mary Hamilton," p. 316; and we shall have occasion to quote some of its variations.—ED.]

THE QUEEN'S MARIE.

Marie Hamilton's to the kirk gane,
　　Wi' ribbons in her hair;
The King thought mair o' Marie Hamilton,
　　Than ony that were there.

Marie Hamilton's to the kirk gane,
　　Wi' ribbons on her breast;
The King thought mair o' Marie Hamilton,
　　Than he listen'd to the priest.

Marie Hamilton's to the kirk gane,
　　Wi' gloves upon her hands;
The King thought mair o' Marie Hamilton,
　　Than the Queen and a' her lands.

She hadna been about the King's court
　　A month, but barely one,
Till she was beloved by a' the King's court,
　　And the King the only man.

She hadna been about the King's court
　　A month, but barely three,

Till frae the King's court Marie Hamilton,
  Marie Hamilton durstna be.

The King is to the Abbey gane,
  To pu' the Abbey tree,
To scale the babe frae Marie's heart;
  But the thing it wadna be.[1]

O she has row'd it in her apron,
  And set it on the sea,—
"Gae sink ye, or swim ye, bonny babe,
  Ye'se get nae mair o' me."—

Word is to the kitchen gane,
  And word is to the ha',
And word is to the noble room,
  Amang the ladyes a',
That Marie Hamilton's brought to bed,
  And the bonny babe's mist and awa'.

---

[1] ["The Prince's bed it was sae saft,
  The spices they were sae fine,
That out of it she could not be
  While she was scarce fifteen.

"She's gane to the garden gay,
  To pu' o' the savin tree;
But for a' that she could say or do,
  The babie it would not die."
          MOTHERWELL, p. 317.]

Scarcely had she lain down again,
  And scarcely fa'en asleep,
When up then started our gude Queen,[1]
  Just at her bed-feet;
Saying—" Marie Hamilton, where's your babe?
  For I am sure I heard it greet."—

" O no, O no, my noble Queen!
  Think no such thing to be;
'Twas but a stitch into my side,
  And sair it troubles me."—[2]

" Get up, get up, Marie Hamilton:
  Get up and follow me;
For I am going to Edinburgh town,
  A rich wedding for to see."—

---

[1] [" Queen Mary cam tripping down the stair,
  Wi' the gold rings in her hair:
' O where is the little babe,' she says,
  ' That I heard greet sae sair?' "
                    MOTHERWELL'S *Version*.]

[2] [" ' There is na babe within my bower,
  And I hope there ne'er will be;
But it's me wi' a sair and sick colic,
  And I'm just like to dee.'

" But they looked up, they looked doun,
  Atween the bowsters and the wa',
It's there they got a bonny lad-bairn,
  But its life it was awa'. "
                    KINLOCH'S *Version*.]

O slowly, slowly raise she up,
   And slowly put she on;
And slowly rode she out the way,
   Wi' mony a weary groan.

The Queen was clad in scarlet,
   Her merry maids all in green;
And every town that they cam to,
   They took Marie for the Queen.

" Ride hooly, hooly, gentlemen,
   Ride hooly now wi' me!
For never, I am sure, a wearier burd
   Rade in your cumpanie."—

But little wist Marie Hamilton,
   When she rade on the brown,
That she was ga'en to Edinburgh town,
   And a' to be put down.

" Why weep ye so, ye burgess wives,
   Why look ye so on me?
O, I am going to Edinburgh town,
   A rich wedding for to see."—[1]

---

[1] [" ' What need ye hech! and how! ladies,
   What need ye how! for me?
Ye never saw grace at a graceless face,—
   Queen Mary has nane to gie.'

When she gaed up the tolbooth stairs,
    The corks frae her heels did flee;
And lang or e'er she cam down again,
    She was condemn'd to die.

When she cam to the Netherbow port,[1]
    She laughed loud laughters three;
But when she cam to the gallows foot,
    The tears blinded her ee.

" Yestreen the Queen had four Maries,
    The night she'll hae but three;
There was Marie Seaton, and Marie Beaton,[2]
    And Marie Carmichael, and me.[3]

    " ' Gae forward, gae forward,' the Queen she said,
      ' Gae forward, that ye may see;
    For the very same words that ye hae said
      Sall hang ye on the gallows tree.' "
                              KINLOCH'S *Version.*]

[1] The Netherbow port was the gate which divided the city of Edinburgh from the suburb, called the Canongate. It had towers and a spire, which formed a fine termination to the view from the Cross. The gate was pulled down in one of those fits of rage for indiscriminate destruction, with which the magistrates of a corporation are sometimes visited.

[2] [At Balfour House, in Fifeshire, there is a full-length portrait of Mary Beaton.—C. K. SHARPE.]

[3] The Queen's Maries were four young ladies of the highest families in Scotland, who were sent to France in her train, and returned with her to Scotland. They are mentioned by Knox, in the quotation introductory to this ballad. Keith gives us their

> "O, often have I dress'd my Queen,
>   And put gold upon her hair;
> But now I've gotten for my reward
>   The gallows to be my share.

names, p. 55. "The young Queen, Mary, embarked at Dunbarton for France, ... , and with her went . . . . . , and four young virgins, all of the name of Mary, viz. Livingston, Fleming, Seatoun, and Beatoun." The Queen's Maries are mentioned again by the same author, p. 288 and 291, in the note. Neither Mary Livingston, nor Mary Fleming, are mentioned in the ballad; nor are the Mary Hamilton, and Mary Carmichael, of the ballad, mentioned by Keith. But if this corps continued to consist of young virgins, as when originally raised, it could hardly have subsisted without occasional recruits; especially if we trust our old bard, and John Knox. The following additional notices of the Queen's Maries, occur in MONTEITH's *Translation of Buchanan's Epigrams, &c.*

Page 60. *Pomp of the Gods at the Marriage of Queen Mary, 29th July, 1565, a Dialogue.*

> DIANA.—" Great father, Maries[1] five late served me,
>   Were of my quire the glorious dignitie;
>   With these dear five the heaven I'd regain,
>   The happiness of other gods to stain;
>   At my lot Juno, Venus, were in ire,
>   And stole away one."———

P. 61. APOLLO.—" Fear not, Diana, I good tidings bring,
  And unto you glad oracles I sing;
  Juno commands your Maries to be married,
  And, in all state, to marriage-bed be carried."

P. 62. JUPITER.—" Five Maries thine:
  One Marie now remains of Delia's five,
  And she at wedlock o'er shortly will arrive."

P. 64. " To Mary Fleming, the King's valentyn—"
    65. " To Mary Beton, Queen by lot, the day before the coronation."
                                    Sundry Verses.

[1] The Queen seems to be included in this number.

"Often have I dress'd my Queen,
  And often made her bed;
But now I've gotten for my reward
  The gallows tree to tread.

"I charge ye all, ye mariners,
  When ye sail ower the faem,
Let neither my father nor mother get wit,
  But that I'm coming hame.

"I charge ye all, ye mariners,
  That sail upon the sea,
Let neither my father nor mother get wit
  This dog's death I'm to die.

"For if my father and mother got wit,
  And my bold brethren three,
O mickle wad be the gude red blude
  This day wad be spilt for me!

"O little did my mother ken,
  That day she cradled me,
The lands I was to travel in,
  Or the death I was to die!"

The Queen's Maries are mentioned in many ballads, and the name seems to have passed into a general denomination for female attendants:—

"Now bear a hand, my Maries a',
And busk me brave, and make me fine."
Old Ballad.

["The *Lament of the Queen's Marie*, connected with its tale, bears so strong a stamp of nature, that we cannot resist quoting it; hoping, at the same time, that Mr Scott will spare no pains to recover the remainder, if there be any."

STODDART, *Edinburgh Review*, January, 1803.

(The reviewer had then only three stanzas to quote, and these, in the order they are now given, were stanzas 23, 18, 19.)

It is evident that Burns had known more of this exquisite old ballad than Mr Scott gave in his first edition of the Minstrelsy. In a letter to Mrs Dunlop, conveying some information about poor Falconer's fate, and dated 25th January, 1795, he introduces the following:—

"Little does the fond mother think, as she hangs delighted over the sweet little leech at her bosom, where the poor fellow may hereafter wander, and what may be his fate. I remember a stanza in an old Scottish ballad, which, notwithstanding its rude simplicity, speaks feelingly to the heart—

'Little did my mother think,
That day she cradled me,
What land I was to travel in,
Or what death I should die.'

"Old Scotch songs are, you know, a favourite study and pursuit of mine; and now I am on that subject, allow me to give you two stanzas of another old simple ballad, which, I am sure, will please you. The catastrophe of the piece is a poor ruined female, lamenting her fate. She concludes with the pathetic wish—

'O that my father had ne'er on me smil'd;
O that my mother had ne'er to me sung
O that my cradle had never been rock'd;
But that I had died when I was young!

'O that the grave it were my bed;
My blankets were my winding-sheet;
The clocks and the worms my bed-fellows a';
And, O, sae sound as I should sleep!'

"I do not remember, in all my reading, to have met with any thing more truly the language of misery, than the exclamation in the last line. Misery is like love; to speak its language truly, the author must have felt it."

BURNS, 8vo, vol. ii. p. 289.—ED.]

THE BONNY HYND.

From Mr HERD's MS., where the following Note is prefixed to it—" Copied from the mouth of a milkmaid, 1771, by W. L."

IT was originally my intention to have omitted this ballad, on account of the disagreeable nature of the subject. Upon consideration, however, it seemed a fair sample of a certain class of songs and tales, turning upon incidents the most horrible and unnatural, with which the vulgar in Scotland are greatly delighted, and of which they have current amongst them an ample store. Such, indeed, are the subjects of composition in most nations, during the early period of society; when the feelings, rude and callous, can only be affected by the strongest stimuli, and where the mind does not, as in a more refined age, recoil, disgusted, from the means by which interest has been excited. Hence incest, parricide—crimes, in fine, the foulest and most enormous, were the early themes of the Grecian muse. Whether that delicacy, which precludes the modern bard from the choice of such impressive and dreadful themes, be favourable to the higher classes of poetic composition, may perhaps be questioned; but there can be little doubt that the more important cause of virtue and morality is advanced by this exclusion. The knowledge, that enormities are not without precedent, may promote, and even suggest them. Hence, the publication of the *Newgate Register* has been prohibited by the wisdom of the legislature, having been found to encourage those very crimes of which it recorded the punishment. Hence, too, the wise maxim of the Romans, *Facinora ostendi dum puniantur, flagitia autem abscondi debent.*

The ballad has a high degree of poetical merit.

THE SCOTTISH BORDER.

THE BONNY HYND.

COPIED

FROM THE MOUTH OF A MILKMAID,

IN 1771.

O May she comes, and May she goes,
   Down by yon gardens green;
And there she spied a gallant squire,
   As squire had ever been.

And May she comes, and May she goes,
   Down by yon hollin tree;
And there she spied a brisk young squire,
   And a brisk young squire was he.

"Give me your green manteel, fair maid;
   Give me your maidenhead![1]
Gin ye winna give me your green manteel,
   Give me your maidenhead!"—

[1] [V. R. It's not for you a weed.—ED.]

. . . . . .

"Perhaps there may be bairns, kind sir;
　Perhaps there may be nane;
But if you be a courtier,
　You'll tell me soon your name."—

"I am nae courtier, fair maid,
　But new come frae the sea;
I am nae courtier, fair maid,
　But when I court with thee.

"They call me Jack, when I'm abroad;
　Sometimes they call me John;
But, when I'm in my father's bower,
　Jock Randal is my name."—

"Ye lee, ye lee, ye bonny lad!
　Sae loud's I hear ye lee!
For I'm Lord Randal's ae daughter,
　He has nae mair nor me."—

¹ [Mr Motherwell gives the following as the stanza here omitted by Herd:—

"He's ta'en her by the milkwhite hand,
　And saftly laid her down;
And when he lifted her up again,
　He gae her a silver kaim.'—ED.]

"Ye lee, ye lee, ye bonny May!
　Sae loud's I hear ye lee!
For I'm Lord Randal's ae ae son,
　Just now come o'er the sea."—

She's putten her hand down by her gare,
　And out she's ta'en a knife;
And she has put it in her heart's bleed,
　And ta'en away her life.¹

And he has ta'en up his bonny sister,
　With the big tear in his een;
And he has buried his bonny sister
　Amang the hollins green.

And syne he's hied him o'er the dale,
　His father dear to see—
"Sing, Oh! and Oh! for my bonny hynd,
　Beneath yon hollin tree!"—

"What needs you care for your bonny hynd?
　For it you needna care;
Take you the best, gie me the warst,
　Since plenty is to spare."—

"I carena for your hynds, my lord,
　I carena for your fee;

¹ [*V. R.* "She's soak'd it in her red heart's blood,
　　　And twined herself of life."—MOTHERWELL.]

But Oh! and Oh! for my bonny hynd,
    Beneath the hollin tree!"—

" O were ye at your sister's bower,
    Your sister fair to see,
You'll think nae mair o' your bonny hynd,
    Beneath the hollin tree."—

* * * * * *

O GIN MY LOVE WERE YON RED ROSE.

FROM MR HERD'S MS.

O gin my love were yon red rose,
   That grows upon the castle wa',
And I mysell a drap of dew,
   Down on that red rose I would fa'.
      O my love's bonny, bonny, bonny;
        My love's bonny, and fair to see;
      Whene'er I look on her weel-far'd face,
        She looks and smiles again to me.

O gin my love were a pickle of wheat,
   And growing upon yon lily lee,
And I mysell a bonny wee bird,
   Awa' wi' that pickle o' wheat I wad flee.
      O my love's bonny, &c.

O gin my love were a coffer o' gowd,
   And I the keeper of the key,

I wad open the kist whene'er I list,
    And in that coffer I wad be.
        O my love's bonny, &c.[1]

[1] [For the originals of all these lover's wishes, see the Greek Anthology, *passim*, or the English translations of Bland and Merivale, 2 vols. 12mo, 1833.—ED.]

O TELL ME HOW TO WOO THEE.

The following verses are taken down from recitation, and are averred to be of the age of CHARLES I. *They have, indeed, much of the romantic expression of passion common to the poets of that period, whose lays still reflected the setting beams of chivalry; but, since their publication in the first edition of this work, the Editor has been assured that they were composed by the late Mr* GRAHAM *of Gartmore.*[1]

If doughty deeds my ladye please,
  Right soon I'll mount my steed;
And strong his arm, and fast his seat,
  That bears frae me the meed.
I'll wear thy colours in my cap,
  Thy picture in my heart;
And he that bends not to thine eye
  Shall rue it to his smart.
    Then tell me how to woo thee, love;
    O tell me how to woo thee!

[1] [When these verses were included in the first edition of the Minstrelsy, Sir W. Scott told me he believed them to have been the composition of a nobler Grahame—the great Marquis of Montrose.—ED.]

For thy dear sake, nae care I'll take,
　　　　Tho' ne'er another trow me.

If gay attire delight thine eye,
　I'll dight me in array;
I'll tend thy chamber door all night,
　And squire thee all the day.
If sweetest sounds can win thy ear,
　These sounds I'll strive to catch;
Thy voice I'll steal to woo thysell,
　That voice that nane can match.
　　　Then tell me how to woo thee, love;
　　　　O tell me how to woo thee!
　　　For thy dear sake, nae care I'll take,
　　　　Tho' ne'er another trow me.

But if fond love thy heart can gain,
　I never broke a vow;
Nae maiden lays her skaith to me,
　I never loved but you.
For you alone I ride the ring,
　For you I wear the blue;
For you alone I strive to sing,
　O tell me how to woo!
　　　O tell me how to woo thee, love;
　　　　O tell me how to woo thee!
　　　For thy dear sake, nae care I'll take,
　　　　Tho' ne'er another trow me.

THE SOUTERS OF SELKIRK.

This little lyric piece, with those which immediately follow in the collection, relates to the fatal battle of Flodden, in which the flower of the Scottish nobility fell around their sovereign, James IV.

The ancient and received tradition of the burgh of Selkirk affirms, that the citizens of that town distinguished themselves by their gallantry on that disastrous occasion. Eighty in number, and headed by their town-clerk, they joined their monarch on his entrance into England. James, pleased with the appearance of this gallant troop, knighted their leader, William Brydone, upon the field of battle, from which few of the men of Selkirk were destined to return. They distinguished themselves in the conflict, and were almost all slain. The few survivors, on their return home, found, by the side of Lady-Wood Edge, the corpse of a female, wife to one of their fallen comrades, with a child sucking at her breast. In memory of this latter event, continues the tradition, the present arms of the burgh bear a female, holding a child in her arms, and seated on a sarcophagus, decorated with the Scottish lion; in the background a wood.

A learned antiquary,[1] whose judgment and accuracy claim respect, has made some observations upon the probability of this tradition, which the Editor shall take the liberty of quoting, as an introduction to what he has to offer upon the same subject. And if he shall have the misfortune to differ from the learned gentleman, he will at least lay candidly before the public the grounds of his opinion.

"That the souters of Selkirk should, in 1513, amount to fourscore fighting men, is a circumstance utterly incredible. It is scarcely to be supposed that all the shoemakers in Scotland could have produced such an army, at a period when shoes must have been still less worn than they are at present. Dr Johnson, indeed, was told at Aberdeen, that the people learned the art of making shoes from Cromwell's soldiers.—' The numbers,' he adds, ' that go barefoot, are still sufficient to show that shoes may be spared; they are not yet considered as necessaries of life; for tall boys, not otherwise meanly dressed, run without them in the streets; and, in the islands, the sons of gentlemen pass several of their first years with naked feet.'—(*Journey to the Western Islands*, p. 55.) Away, then, with the fable of the Souters of Selkirk! Mr Tytler, though he mentions it as the subject of a song, or ballad, ' does not remember ever to have seen the original genuine words,'— as he obligingly acknowledged in a letter to the Editor.

---

[1] [The late Mr Joseph Ritson.]

Mr Robertson, however, who gives the Statistical Account of the Parish of Selkirk, seems to know something more of the matter.—' Some,' says he, ' have *very falsely* attributed to this event (the battle of Flowden,) that song,

> ' Up wi' the souters of Selkirk,
> And down with the Earl of Home.'

"' There was no Earl of Home,' he adds, ' at that time, nor was this song composed till long after. It arose from a bet betwixt the Philiphaugh and Home families; the souters (or shoemakers) of Selkirk, against the men of Home, at a match of football, in which the souters of Selkirk completely gained, and afterwards perpetuated their victory in that song.' This is decisive; and so much for Scottish tradition."—Note to *Historical Essay on Scottish Song*, prefixed to *Scottish Songs*, in 2 vols. 1794.

It is proper to remark, that the passage of Mr Robertson's Statistical Account, above quoted, does not relate to the authenticity of the tradition, but to the origin of the song, which is obviously a separate and distinct question. The entire passage in the Statistical Account (of which a part only is quoted in the essay) runs thus:—

" Here, too, the inhabitants of the town of Selkirk, who breathed the manly spirit of real freedom, justly merit particular attention. Of one hundred citizens, who followed the fortunes of James IV. on the plains of Flowden, a few returned, loaded with the spoils taken from the enemy. Some of these trophies still survive the rust of time, and the effects of negligence. The desperate valour of the citizens of Selkirk, which, on that fatal day, was eminently conspicuous to both armies, produced very opposite effects. The implacable resentment of the English reduced their defenceless town to ashes; while their grateful sovereign (James V.) showed his sense of their valour, by a grant of an extensive portion of the forest, the trees for building their houses, and the property as the reward of their heroism."—A note is added by Mr Robertson.—" A standard, the appearance of which bespeaks its antiquity, is still carried annually (on the day of riding their common) by the corporation of weavers, by a member of which it was taken from the English in the field of Flowden. It may be added, that the sword of William Brydone, the town-clerk, who led the citizens to the battle, (and who is said to have been knighted for his valour,) is still in the possession of John Brydone, a citizen of Selkirk, his lineal descendant."—An additional note contains the passage quoted in the *Essay on Scottish Song.*

If the testimony of Mr Robertson is to be received as decisive of the question, the learned author of the essay will surely admit, upon re-perusal, that the passage in the Statistical Account contains the most positive and unequivocal declaration of his belief in the tradition.

Neither does the story itself, upon close examination, contain any thing inconsistent with probability. The towns upon the Border, and especially Selkirk and Jedburgh, were inhabited by a race of citizens, who, from the necessity of their situation, and from the nature of their possessions, (held by burgage tenure,) were inured to the use of arms. Selkirk was a county town, and a royal burgh; and when the array of the kingdom, amounting to no less than one hundred thousand warriors, was marshalled by the royal command, eighty men seems no unreasonable proportion from a place of consequence, lying so very near the scene of action.

Neither is it necessary to suppose, literally, that the men of Selkirk were all *souters*. This appellation was obviously bestowed on them, because it was the trade most generally practised in the town, and therefore passed into a general epithet. Even the existence of such a craft, however, is accounted improbable by the learned essayist, who seems hardly to allow, that the Scottish nation was, at that period, acquainted with the art " of accommodating their feet with shoes." And here he attacks us with our own weapons, and wields the tradition of Aberdeen against that of Selkirk. We shall not stop to enquire, in what respect Cromwell's regiment of missionary cobblers deserves, in point of probability, to take precedence of the souters of Selkirk. But, allowing that all the shoemakers in England, with *Praise-the-Lord Barebones* at their head, had generously combined to instruct the men of Aberdeen in the arts of psalmody and cobbling, it by no means bears upon the present question. If instruction was at all necessary, it must have been in teaching the natives how to make *shoes*, properly so called, in opposition to *brogues:* For there were cordiners in Aberdeen long before Cromwell's visit, and several fell in the battle of the Bridge of Dee, as appears from Spalding's *History of the Troubles in Scotland*, vol. ii. p. 140. Now, the " single-soled shoon," made by the souters of Selkirk, were a sort of brogues, with a single thin sole; the purchaser himself performing the farther operation of sewing on another of thick leather. The rude and imperfect state of this manufacture sufficiently evinces the antiquity of the craft. Thus, the profession of the citizens of Selkirk, instead of invalidating, confirms the traditional account of their valour.

The total devastation of this unfortunate burgh, after the fatal battle of Flodden, is ascertained by the charters under which the corporation hold their privileges. The first of these is granted by James V., and is dated 4th March, 1535-6. The narrative or inductive clause of the deed, is in these words: " *Sciatis quia nos considerantes et intelligentes quod Carte Evidencie et litere veteris fundacionis et infeofamenti burgi nostri de Selkirk et libertatum ejusdem burgensibus et communitati ipsius per nobilissimos progenitores nostros quorum animabus propicietur Deus dat. et concess. per guerrarum assultus pestem combustionem et alias pro majore parte vastantur et distruuntur unde mercantiarum usus inter ipsos burgenses cessavit in eorum magnam lesionem ac reipublice et libertatis Burgi nostri antedict. destruccionem et prejudicium ac ingens nobis dampnum penes nostras Custumas et firmas burgales ab eodem nobis debit. si subitum in eisdem remedium minime habitum fuerit—NOS igitur pietate et justicia moti ac pro policia et edificiis infra regnum nostrum habend. de novo infeodamus,*" &c. The charter proceeds, in common form, to erect anew the town of Selkirk into a royal burgh, with all the privileges annexed to such corporations. This mark of royal favour was confirmed by a second charter, executed by the same monarch, after he had attained the age of majority, and dated April 8, 1538. This deed of confirmation first narrates the charter, which has been already quoted, and then proceeds to mention other grants, which had been conferred upon the burgh, during the minority of James V., and which are thus expressed: " We for the gude trew and thankful service done and to be done to ws be owre lovittis the baillies burgesses and communite of our burgh of Selkirk and for certain otheris reasonable causis and considerationis moving ws be the tennor hereof grantis and gevis license to thame and their successors to ryfe out breke and teil yeirlie une thousand [1] acres of their common landis of our said

[1] It is probable that Mr Robertson had not seen this deed,

burgh in what part thairof thea pleas for polecy
strengthing and bigging of the samyn for the wele of
ws and of lieges repairand thairto and defence againis
owre auld innemyis of Ingland and other wayis and
will and grantis that thai sall nocht be callit accusit
nor incur ony danger or skaith thairthrow in thair
personis landis nor gudes in ony wise in time coming
NOCHTWITHSTANDING ony owre actis or statutis maid
or to be maid in the contrar in ony panys contenit
tharein anent the quhilkis we dispens with thame be
thir owre letters with power to them to occupy the
saidis landis with thare awne gudis or to set theme to
tenentis as thai sall think maist expedient for the wele
of our said burgh with frei ische and entri and with all
and sindry utheris commoditeis freedomes asiamentis
and richtuis pertenentis whatsumever pertenyng or that
rychtuisly may pertene thairto perpetually in tyme
cuming frelie quietlie wele and in peace but ony revo-
catioun or agane calling whatsumever Gevin under
owre signet and subscrivit with owre hand at Strive-

---

when he wrote his Statistical Account of the Parish of Selkirk;
for it appears, that, instead of a grant of lands, the privilege granted
to the community was a right of tilling one thousand acres of those
which already belonged to the burgh. Hence it follows, that, previous to the field of Flodden, the town must have been possessed of
a spacious domain, to which a thousand acres in tillage might bear
a due proportion. This circumstance ascertains the antiquity and
power of the burgh; for, had this large tract of land been granted
during the minority of James V., the donation, to be effectual,
most have been included in the charters of confirmation.

ling the twenty day of Junii The yere of God ane thousand five hundreth and thretty six yeris and of our regne the twenty thre year." Here follows another grant: "We UNDERSTANDING that owre burgh of Selkirk and inhabitants thairof CONTINUALIE SEN THE FIELD OF FLODOUNE has been oppressiit heriit and owre runin be theves and traitors whairthrow the haunt of merchandice has cessit amangis thame of langtyme bygane and thai heriit thairtbrow and we defraudit of owre custumis and dewites—THAIRFOR and for divers utheris resonable causis and consliderationes moving us be the tenor heirof of our kinglie power fre motive and autoritie ryall grantis and givis to thame and thair successors ane fair day begynand at the feist of the Conception of owre Lady next to cum aftere the day of the date hereof and be the octavis of the sammyn perpetualy in time cuming To be usit and exercit be thame als frelie in time cuming as ony uther fair is usit or exercit be ony otheris owre burrowis within owre realme payand yeirlie custumis and doweities sucht and wont as effeiris frelie quietlie wele and in pece but ony revocation obstakill impediment or agane calling whatsumever Subscrivet with owre hand and gevin under owre Signet at KIRKALDY the secund day of September The yere of God ane thousand five hundreth and threty sex yeris and of owre regne the twenty three yeir." The charter of confirmation, in which all these deeds and letters of donation are engrossed, proceeds to ratify and confirm them in the most ample manner. The testing clause, as it is termed in law language, is in these words: "*In cujus rei Testimonium huic presente carte nostre confirmationis magnum sigillum nostrum apponi precepimus* TESTIBUS *Reverendissimo reverendisque in Christo Patribus Gawino Archiepisco. Glasguen. Cancellario nostro; Georgio Episcopo Dunkelden. Henrico Episcopo Candide Case nostreque Capelle regie Strivilengen. decano; dilectis nostris consanguineis Jacobo Moravie Comite, &c. Archibaldo Comite de Ergile Domino Campbell et Lorne Magistro Hospicii nostri, Hugone Comite de Eglinton Domino Montgomery, Malcolmo Domino Flemyng magno Camerario nostro, Venerabilibus in Christo Patribus Patricio Priore Ecclesie Metropolitane Sanctiandree, Alexandro Abbate Monasterii nostri de Cambuskynneth—dilectis familiaribus nostris Thomæ Erskin de Brechin, Secretario nostro Jacobo Colville de Estwemis compotorum nostrorum rotulatore et nostre cancellarie directore, militibus, et Magistro Jacobo Foulis de Colintoun nostrorum rotulorum Registri et Concilii clerico—apud Edinburgh octavo die mensis Aprilis Anno Domini millesimo quingentesimo trigesimo octavo et regni nostri vicesimo quinto.*"

From these extracts, which are accurately copied from the original charters,[1] it may be safely concluded, 1st, that Selkirk was a place of importance before it

---

[1] The charters are preserved in the records of the burgh.

was ruined by the English; and, 2d, "that the voice of merchants had ceased in her streets," in consequence of the fatal field of Flodden. But further, it seems reasonable to infer, that so many marks of royal favour, granted within so short a time of each other, evince the gratitude, as well as the compassion, of the monarch, and were intended to reward the valour, as well as to relieve the distress, of the men of Selkirk. Thus every circumstance of the written evidence, as far as it goes, tallies with the oral tradition of the inhabitants; and, therefore, though the latter may be exaggerated, it surely cannot be dismissed as entirely void of foundation. That William Brydone actually enjoyed the honour of knighthood, is ascertained by many of the deeds, in which his name appears as a notary-public. John Brydone, lineal descendant of the gallant town-clerk, is still alive, and possessed of the relics mentioned by Mr Robertson. The old man, though in an inferior station of life, receives considerable attention from his fellow-citizens, and claims no small merit to himself on account of his brave ancestor.[1]

Thus far concerning the tradition of the exploits of the men of Selkirk, at Flodden field. Whether the following verses do, or do not, bear any allusion to that event, is a separate and less interesting question. The

---

[1] This person is lately dead, but his son is in possession of the weapons in question. 1810.

opinion of Mr Robertson, referring them to a different origin, has been already mentioned; but his authority, though highly respectable, is not absolutely decisive of the question.

The late Mr Plummer,[1] sheriff-depute of the county of Selkirk, a faithful and accurate antiquary, entertained a very opposite opinion. He has thus expressed himself upon the subject, in the course of his literary correspondence with Mr Herd :—

" Of the Souters of Selkirk, I never heard any words but the following verse :

> ' Up with the Souters of Selkirk,
>   And down wi' the Earl of Home;
> And up wi' a' the bra' lads
>   That sew the single-soled shoon.'

" It is evident that these words cannot be so ancient as to come near the time when the battle was fought; as Lord Home was not created an Earl till near a century after that period.

" Our clergyman, in the ' Statistical Account,' vol. ii. p. 48, note, says, that these words were composed upon a match at foot-ball, between the Philiphaugh and Home families. I was five years at school at Selkirk, have lived all my days within two miles of that town, and never once heard a tradition of this imaginary contest till I saw it in print.

[1] [Andrew Plummer, Esq., of Sunderland Hall, Selkirkshire.— ED.]

"Although the words are not very ancient, there is every reason to believe, that they allude to the battle of Flodden, and to the different behaviour of the souters, and Lord Home, upon that occasion. At election dinners, &c., when the Selkirk folks begin to get *fou'* (merry), they always call for music, and for that tune in particular.[1] At such times I never heard a souter hint at the foot-ball, but many times speak of the battle of Flodden."—*Letter from Mr Plummer to Mr Herd, 13th January,* 1793.

The Editor has taken every opportunity, which his situation[2] has afforded him, to obtain information on this point, and has been enabled to recover two additional verses of the song.

The yellow and green, mentioned in the second verse, are the liveries of the house of Home. When the Lord Home came to attend the governor, Albany, his attendants were arrayed in Kendal-green.—GODSCROFT.

[1] A singular custom is observed at conferring the freedom of the burgh. Four or five bristles, such as are used by shoemakers, are attached to the seal of the burgess ticket. These the new-made burgess must dip in his wine, and pass through his mouth, in token of respect for the souters of Selkirk. This ceremony is on no account dispensed with.

[2] That the Editor succeeded Mr Plummer in his office of sheriff-depute, and has himself the honour to be a souter of Selkirk, may perhaps form the best apology for the length of this dissertation.

THE SOUTERS OF SELKIRK.

Up wi' the Souters of Selkirk,
    And down wi' the Earl of Home;
And up wi' a' the braw lads,
    That sew the single-soled shoon.

Fye upon yellow and yellow,
    And fye upon yellow and green,
But up wi' the true blue and scarlet,
    And up wi' the single-soled sheen.

Up wi' the Souters o' Selkirk,
    For they are baith trusty and leal;
And up wi' the Men o' the Forest,[1]
    And down wi' the Merse[2] to the deil.[3]

---

[1] Selkirkshire, otherwise called Ettrick Forest.

[2] Berwickshire, otherwise called the Merse.

[3] It is unnecessary here to enter into a formal refutation of the popular calumny, which taxed Lord Home with being the murderer of his sovereign, and the cause of the defeat at Flodden. So far from exhibiting any marks of cowardice or disaffection, the division headed by that unfortunate nobleman, was the only part of the Scottish army which was conducted with common prudence on

that fatal day. This body formed the vanguard, and entirely routed the division of Sir Edmund Howard, to which they were opposed; but the reserve of the English cavalry rendered it impossible for Home, notwithstanding his success, to come to the aid of the king, who was irretrievably ruined by his own impetuosity of temper.—PINKERTON's *History*, vol. ii. p. 105. The escape of James from the field of battle has long been deservedly ranked with that of King Sebastian, and similar *speciosa miracula* with which the vulgar have been amused in all ages. Indeed, the Scottish nation were so very unwilling to admit any advantage on the English part, that they seem actually to have set up pretensions to the victory.[1] The same temper of mind led them eagerly to ascribe the loss of their monarch, and his army, to any cause, rather than to his own misconduct, and the superior military skill of the English. There can be no doubt, that James actually fell on the field of battle, the slaughter-place of his nobles.—PINKERTON, *ibid*. His dead body was interred in the monastery of Sheen, in Surrey; and Stowe mentions, with regard to it, the following degrading circumstances:—

"After the battle the bodie of the said king, being found, was closed in lead, and conveyed from thence to London, and to the monasterie of Sheyne, in Surry, where it remained for a time, in what order I am not certaine; but, since the dissolution of that house, in the reign of Edward VI., Henry Gray, Duke of Norfolke, being lodged, and keeping house there, I have been shewed the same bodie, so lapped in lead, close to the head and bodie, throwne into

[1] " Against the proud Scotte's clattering,
That never wyll leave their trattlying;
Wan they the field and lost theyr king?
They may well say, fie on that winning!

" Lo these fond sottes and trattlying Scottes,
How they are blinde in their own minde,
And will not know theyr overthrow.
At Branxton moore they are so stowre,
So frantike mad, and say they had,
And wan the field with speare and shielde:
That is as true as black is blue," &c.
Skelton Laureate against the Scottes.

a waste room, amongst the old timber, lead, and other rubble. Since the which time, workmen there, for their foolish pleasure, hewed off his head; and Lancelot Young, master glazier to Queen Elizabeth, feeling a sweet savour to come from thence, and seeing the same dried from all moisture, and yet the form remaining, with haires of the head, and beard red, brought it to London, to his house in Wood-street, where, for a time, he kept it, for its sweetness, but, in the end, caused the sexton of that church (St Michael's, Wood-street) to bury it amongst other bones taken out of their charnel."—STOWE's *Surrey of London*, p. 539.

THE FLOWERS OF THE FOREST.

PART FIRST.

The following well-known and beautiful stanzas were composed, many years ago, by a lady of family in Roxburghshire. The manner of the ancient minstrels is so happily imitated, that it required the most positive evidence to convince the Editor that the song was of modern date. Such evidence, however, he has been able to procure; having been favoured, through the kind intervention of Dr Somerville (well known to the literary world, as the historian of King William, &c.), with the following authentic copy of the *Flowers of the Forest.*

From the same respectable authority, the Editor is enabled to state, that the tune of the ballad is ancient, as well as the two following lines of the first stanza:—

I've heard them lilting at the ewes milking,
— — — — —
— — — — —
The flowers of the forest are a' wede away.

Some years after the song was composed, a lady, who is now dead, repeated to the author another imperfect line of the original ballad, which presents a simple and affecting image to the mind :—

> " I ride single on my saddle,
> For the flowers of the forest are a' wede away."

The first of these trifling fragments, joined to the remembrance of the fatal battle of Flodden, (in the calamities accompanying which the inhabitants of Ettrick Forest' suffered a distinguished share,) and to the present solitary and desolate appearance of the country, excited, in the mind of the author, the ideas, which she has expressed in a strain of elegiac simplicity and tenderness, which has seldom been equalled.

THE FLOWERS OF THE FOREST.

PART FIRST.

I've heard them lilting,[1] at the ewe-milking,
    Lasses a' lilting, before dawn of day;
But now they are moaning on ilka green loaning;
    The flowers of the forest are a' wede awae.

At bughts, in the morning, nae blythe lads are scorning;
    Lasses are lonely, and dowie, and wae;
Nae daffing, nae gabbing, but sighing and sabbing;
    Ilk ane lifts her leglin, and hies her awae.

In har'st, at the shearing, nae youths now are jeering;
    Bandsters are runkled, and lyart or gray;

---

[1] The following explanation of provincial terms may be found useful.

Lilting—Singing cheerfully. *Loaning*—A broad lane. *Wede awae*—Weeded out. *Scorning*—Rallying. *Dowie*—Dreary. *Daffing and gabbing*—Joking and chatting. *Leglin*—Milk-pail. *Har'st*—Harvest. *Shearing*—Reaping. *Bandsters*—Sheaf-binders. *Runkled*—Wrinkled. *Lyart*—Inclining to grey. *Fleeching*—Coaxing. *Gloaming*—Twilight.

At fair, or at preaching,[1] nae wooing, nae fleeching;
  The flowers of the forest are a' wede awae.

At e'en, in the gloaming, nae younkers are roaming
  'Bout stacks with the lasses at bogle to play;
But ilk maid sits dreary, lamenting her deary—
  The flowers of the forest are weded awae.

Dool and wae for the order, sent our lads to the Border!
  The English, for ance, by guile wan the day:
The flowers of the forest, that fought aye the foremost,
  The prime of our land, are cauld in the clay.

We'll hear nae mair lilting, at the ewe-milking;
  Women and bairns are heartless and wae:

---

[1] These lines have been said to contain an anachronism; the supposed date of the lamentation being about the period of the Field of Flodden. The Editor can see no ground for this charge. Fairs were held in Scotland from the most remote antiquity; and are, from their very nature, scenes of pleasure and gallantry. The preachings of the friars were, indeed, professedly, meetings for a graver purpose; but we have the authority of the *Wife of Bath*, (surely most unquestionable in such a point,) that they were frequently perverted to places of rendezvous :—

> "I had the better leisur for to plaie,
> And for to see, and eke to be scle
> Of lusty folk. What wist I where my grace
> Was shapen for to be, or in what place
> Therefore I made my visitations
> To vigilies and to processions;
> *To preachings eke*, and to thise pilgrimages,
> To playes of miracles, and marriages," &c.
>   *Canterbury Tales.*

Sighing and moaning on ilka green loaning—
The flowers of the forest are a' wede awae.¹

¹ ["It is the business of poetry to delineate feeling; and where shall we look for feeling so undisguised and powerful, as in those early periods of civilisation, which have already excited men to the cultivation of their intellectual energies—but have not yet fettered them with that multiplicity of rules which forms them into the mere machines of polished society? The minds of men in such a state are indeed less delicate, less attractive of general sympathy, than in succeeding periods; but they are more poetic, more interesting in particular contemplation, more distinctly marked and intelligible. We are not, then, to view these poems as *facta ad unguem*—high-polished and elaborate specimens of art—but as exhibiting the true sparks and flashes of individual nature. Hence we shall find a savage wildness in the superstition of the *Lyke-wake Dirge*, and in the tumultuous rage of the *Fray of Suport*; but we may trace gradations from these to the exquisite tenderness of the *Flowers of the Forest*."—*Edin. Rev.* 1803.]

THE FLOWERS OF THE FOREST.

PART SECOND.

The following verses, adapted to the ancient air of the *Flowers of the Forest*, are, like the elegy which precedes them, the production of a lady. The late Mrs Cockburn, daughter of Rutherford of Fairnalie, in Selkirkshire, and relict of Mr Cockburn of Ormiston, (whose father was Lord Justice-Clerk of Scotland,) was the authoress. Mrs Cockburn has been dead but a few years.[1] Even at an age, advanced beyond the usual bounds of humanity, she retained a play of imagination, and an activity of intellect, which must have been attractive and delightful in youth, but were almost preternatural at her period of life. Her active benevolence, keeping pace with her genius, rendered her equally an object of love and admiration. The Editor, who knew her well, takes this opportunity of doing justice to his own feelings; and they are in

[1] Edition of 1803.

unison with those of all who knew his regretted friend.[1]

The verses which follow were written at an early period of life, and without peculiar relation to any event, unless it were the depopulation of Ettrick Forest.

---

[1] [Mrs Cockburn was an intimate friend of Mrs Scott, and among the first persons who discovered the expanding genius of her son.—ED.]

THE FLOWERS OF THE FOREST.

PART SECOND.

I've seen the smiling of Fortune beguiling,
    I've tasted her favours, and felt her decay:
Sweet is her blessing, and kind her caressing,
    But soon it is fled—it is fled far away.

I've seen the forest adorn'd of the foremost,
    With flowers of the fairest, both pleasant and gay;
Full sweet was their blooming, their scent the air perfuming,
    But now are they wither'd, and a' wede awae.

I've seen the morning with gold the hills adorning,
    And the red storm roaring, before the parting day:
I've seen Tweed's silver streams, glittering in the sunny beams,
    Turn drumly[1] and dark, as they roll'd on their way.

O fickle Fortune! why this cruel sporting?
    Why thus perplex us poor sons of a day?
Thy frowns cannot fear me, thy smiles cannot cheer me,
    Since the flowers of the forest are a' wede awae.

[1] *Drumly*—Discoloured.

THE LAIRD OF MUIRHEAD.

This Ballad is a fragment from Mr HERD's MS., *communicated to him by* J. GROSSETT MUIRHEAD, *Esq. of Breadesholm, near Glasgow; who stated that he extracted it, as relating to his own family, from the complete Song, in which the names of twenty or thirty gentlemen were mentioned, contained in a large Collection, belonging to* Mr ALEXANDER MONRO, *merchant in Lisbon, but supposed now to be lost.*

It appears, from the Appendix to NISBET's *Heraldry, p. 264, that* MUIRHEAD *of Lachop and Bullis, the person here called the Laird of* MUIRHEAD, *was a man of rank, being rentaller, or perhaps feuar, of many crown lands in Galloway; and was, in truth, slain in* "Campo Belli de Northumberland sub vexillo Regis," *i. e. in the Field of Flodden.*

. . . . .

AFORE the King in order stude
   The stout laird of Muirhead,
Wi' that same twa-hand muckle sword
   That Bartram fell'd stark dead.

He sware he wadna lose his right
　To fight in ilka field;
Nor budge him from his liege's sight,
　Till his last gasp should yield.

Twa hunder mair, of his ain name,
　Frae Torwood and the Clyde,
Sware they would never gang to hame,
　But a' die by his syde.

And wondrous weel they kept their troth;
　This sturdy royal band
Rush'd down the brae, wi' sic a pith,
　That nane could them withstand.

Mony a bloody blow they dealt,
　The like was never seen;
And hadna that braw leader fall'n,
　They ne'er had slain the king.

ODE

ON VISITING FLODDEN

BY J. LEYDEN.[1]

GREEN FLODDEN! on thy blood-stain'd head
   Descend no rain nor vernal dew;
But still, thou charnel of the dead,
   May whitening bones thy surface strew!
Soon as I tread thy rush-clad vale,
   Wild fancy feels the clasping mail;
The rancour of a thousand years
   Glows in my breast; again I burn
   To see the banner'd pomp of war return,
And mark, beneath the moon, the silver light of spears.

Lo! bursting from their common tomb,
   The spirits of the ancient dead

---

[1] [These verses of Dr Leyden appear to have been introduced in this place, as forming a sort of *note* on the Flowers of the Forest. Among them are the four beautiful lines which were selected for the motto to Marmion—
   " Alas! that Scottish maid should sing," &c.
                                                ED.]

Dimly streak the parted gloom
    With awful faces, ghastly red ;
As once, around their martial king,
They closed the death-devoted ring,
With dauntless hearts, unknown to yield ;
    In slow procession round the pile
Of heaving corses, moves each shadowy file,
And chants, in solemn strain, the dirge of Flodden field.

What youth, of graceful form and mien,
    Foremost leads the spectred brave,
While o'er his mantle's folds of green
    His amber locks redundant wave?
When slow returns the fated day,
That view'd their chieftain's long array,
Wild to the harp's deep plaintive string,
    The virgins raise the funeral strain,
From Ord's black mountain to the northern main,
And mourn the emerald hue which paints the vest of spring.[1]

[1] Under the vigorous administration of James IV., the young Earl of Caithness incurred the penalty of outlawry and forfeiture, for revenging an ancient feud. On the evening preceding the battle of Flodden, accompanied by 300 young warriors, arrayed in green, he presented himself before the King, and submitted to his mercy. This mark of attachment was so agreeable to that warlike prince, that he granted an immunity to the Earl and all his followers. The parchment on which this immunity was inscribed, is said to be still preserved in the archives of the Earls of Caithness, and is marked with the drum-strings, having been cut out of a drum-

Alas! that Scottish maid should sing
  The combat where her lover fell!
That Scottish bard should wake the string,
  The triumph of our foes to tell!
Yet Teviot's sons, with high disdain,
Have kindled at the thrilling strain,
That mourn'd their martial fathers' bier;
  And at the sacred font, the priest
  Through ages left the master-hand unblest,[1]
To urge, with keener aim, the blood-encrusted spear.

Red Flodden! when thy plaintive strain
  In early youth rose soft and sweet,
My life-blood, through each throbbing vein,
  With wild tumultuous passion beat;

head, as no other parchment could be found in the army. The Earl and his gallant band perished to a man in the battle of Flodden; since which period, it has been reckoned unlucky in Caithness to wear *green*, or *cross the Ord on a Monday*, the day of the week on which the Chieftain advanced into Sutherland.

[1] In the Border counties of Scotland, it was formerly customary, when any rancorous enmity subsisted between two clans, to leave the right hand of male children unchristened, that it might deal the more deadly, or, according to the popular phrase, "unhallowed" blows to their enemies. By this superstitious rite, they were devoted to bear the family feud, or enmity. The same practice subsisted in Ireland, as appears from the following passage in CHAMPION's *History of Ireland*, published in 1633. "In some corners of the land they used a damnable superstition, leaving the right armes of their infants, males, unchristened, (as they termed it,) to the end it might give a more ungracious and deadly blow."—P. 15.

And oft, in fancied might, I trode
The spear-strewn path to Fame's abode,
Encircled with a sanguine flood;
And thought I heard the mingling hum,
When, croaking hoarse, the birds of carrion come
Afar, on rustling wing, to feast on English blood.

Rude Border Chiefs, of mighty name,
   And iron soul, who sternly tore
The blossoms from the tree of fame,
   And purpled deep their tints with gore,
Rush from brown ruins, scarr'd with age,
That frown o'er haunted Hermitage;
Where, long by spells mysterious bound,
   They pace their round, with lifeless smile,
   And shake, with restless foot, the guilty pile,
Till sink the mouldering towers beneath the burden'd
     ground.[1]

Shades of the dead! on Alfer's plain
   Who scorned with backward step to move,
But struggling 'mid the hills of slain,
   Against the Sacred Standard strove;[2]

---

[1] Popular superstition in Scotland still retains so formidable an idea of the *guilt of blood*, that those ancient edifices, or castles, where enormous crimes have been committed, are supposed to sink gradually into the ground. With regard to the castle of Hermitage, in particular, the common people believe, that thirty feet of the walls sunk, thirty feet fell, and thirty feet remain standing.

[2] The fatal battle of the Standard was fought on Cowton Moor,

Amid the lanes of war I trace
　　Each broad claymore and ponderous mace :
Where'er the surge of arms is tost,
　　Your glittering spears, in close array,
　　Sweep, like the spider's filmy web, away
The flower of Norman pride, and England's victor host.

But distant fleets each warrior ghost,
　　With surly sounds that murmur far ;
Such sounds were heard when Syria's host
　　Roll'd from the walls of proud Samàr.
Around my solitary head
Gleam the blue lightnings of the dead,
While murmur low the shadowy band—
　　" Lament no more the warrior's doom !
　　Blood, blood alone, should dew the hero's tomb,
Who falls, 'mid circling spears, to save his native land."

near Northallerton, (A. S. Ealfertun,) in Yorkshire, 1138.
David I. commanded the Scottish army. He was opposed by
Thurston, Archbishop of York, who, to animate his followers, had
recourse to the impressions of religious enthusiasm. The mast of
a ship was fitted into the perch of a four-wheeled carriage ; on its
top was placed a little casket, containing a consecrated host. It
also contained the banner of St Cuthbert, round which were displayed those of St Peter of York, St John of Beverley, and St
Wilfred of Rippon. This was the English standard, and was
stationed in the centre of the army. Prince Henry, son of David,
at the head of the men-of-arms, chiefly from Cumberland and Teviotdale, charged, broke, and completely dispersed the centre ; but
unfortunately was not supported by the other divisions of the Scottish army. The expression of Alfred, (p. 345,) describing this

encounter, is more spirited than the general tenor of monkish historians ;—" *Ipsa globi australis parte instar cassis aranea dissipata*"—that division of the phalanx was dispersed like a cobweb.

END OF VOLUME THIRD.

www.ingramcontent.com/pod-product-compliance
Lightning Source LLC
Chambersburg PA
CBHW020320240426
43673CB00039B/868